Leslee Elliott

Sterling Publishing Co., Inc.
New York

With Love To
Stefie, Who Fancies Furry Fellows,
and
Scott, Who Collects Creepy Crawlies

Edited by Dr. Nancy B. Simmons, Assistant Curator
Department of Mammalogy, American Museum of Natural History

Designed by Judy Morgan

1 3 5 7 9 10 8 6 4 2

Published in paperback 2001 by Sterling Publishing Company, Inc.
387 Park Avenue South, New York, N.Y. 10016
Originally published in hard cover as
Mind-Blowing Mammals and *Really Radical Reptiles* © 1994 by Leslee Elliott
Distributed in Canada by Sterling Publishing
c/o Canadian Manda Group, One Atlantic Avenue, Suite 105
Toronto, Ontario, Canada M6K 3E7
Distributed in Great Britain and Europe by Chris Lloyd at Orca Book
Services, Stanley House, Fleets Lane, Poole BH15 3AJ, England.
Distributed in Australia by Capricorn Link (Australia) Pty. Ltd.
P.O. Box 704, Windsor, NSW 2756 Australia

Printed in China

Sterling ISBN 0-8069-9740-0

CONTENTS

Reptiles and Amphibians 67

MIND-BLOWING MAMMALS

SLOW LORIS
Nycticebus coucang

Nancy Adams, TOM STACK AND ASSOCIATES

CAMEL *Dromedary—Camelus dromedrius*

MAM-MAL a warm-blooded, air-breathing animal that feeds its young with milk, has a backbone, two pairs of limbs and usually a covering, more or less, of hair.

But that's not all!

There are actually three different kinds of mammals:

MONOTREMES

3 species, including platypuses and spiny anteaters.

The most primitive animals that can still be called mammals, monotremes still have some things in common with reptiles. For example, they lay eggs.

MARSUPIALS

250 species, including kangaroos, koalas and opossums.

Born in a very immature state, marsupials finish developing in a pouch in their mother's belly.

PLACENTALS

3,755 species, including dogs, horses and whales.

Placentals develop to an advanced state before birth. Some can even stand and run within minutes of their arrival.

Tom Stack, TOM STACK AND ASSOCIATES

ASIAN LION *Panthera leo*

Gary Milburn, TOM STACK AND ASSOCIATES

GALAGO (Bush baby) *Euoticus elegantulus*

MAMMALS EVERYWHERE

Mammals are everywhere—living on the ground like anteaters and antelopes; under it like rodents and rabbits; over it like bats; and even in the water like whales and walruses. Each one of these 4,008 species has something unique about its home, personality or lifestyle. This special something has developed so that the animal may survive successfully in the place, way or style that it does. Sometimes the trait may seem useless or bizarre, until we look further to see why it has developed.

Did the animal need flat teeth to grind plants or sharp teeth to bite meat? Colorful markings to attract attention or drab coloring to hide itself? Sharp claws to fight or strong legs for flight? Long thin arms to swing through the trees or flippers to swim through the sea?

For every obvious advantage, there are curiosities that even scientists cannot figure out. Why do you suppose that only the male platypus has a poison-spur, and why in such an out-of-the-way place as his back leg? Was there an ancient adversary, now extinct, that he had to defend against?

There is a lot left to find out. The more fascinating facts we learn about the mind-blowing mammals, the more questions we have. Perhaps one day you'll be the one to uncover the answers to some of nature's most tantalizing riddles!

WOULD YOU BELIEVE . . .

Humans snore lying down, HORSES standing up!

Young DEER and OTTER play "Hide and Seek," but not together!

In a herd of WILDEBEESTS, all the pregnant females get together for a mass birth event!

BEAVERS' teeth are orange!

You'd need twelve GOATS to replace the milk from one COW!

Pampered CATS in ancient Egypt wore earrings!

In the long run, DOG teams are faster than HORSES!

SEA LIONS actually walk on their flippers!

All MAMMALS crave salt!

Exchanging a kiss is how PRAIRIE DOGS recognize accepted members of their community!

PRAIRIE DOG *Cynomys ludovicianus*

Diana Stratton, TOM STACK AND ASSOCIATES

AND BESIDES THAT, DID YOU KNOW . . .

Thomas Kitchin, TOM STACK AND ASSOCIATES

PORCUPINE *Erethizon dorsatum*

CATS use their whiskers to feel their way in the dark!

The bacteria from the 50 million skin cells humans lose every day are what a tracking BLOODHOUND smells!

Easter Island is home to 4,000 wild HORSES and only 3,000 humans!

Contented BRAHMA BULLS purr!

The SPRINGBOK ANTELOPE can bounce straight up 12 feet (3.6m) in the air!

Bee-sting and snake-bite can't penetrate the HONEY BADGER's skin!

Cat connoisseurs claim the BOBCAT is braver than the LYNX!

In a dive, BEAVERS can swim about half a mile (800m) on one gulp of air!

PORCUPINES have as many as 30,000 spiny quills!

Joe McDonald, TOM STACK AND ASSOCIATES

AFRICAN ELEPHANT *Loxodonta africans*

SOME GIANTS ARE STILL HERE

In prehistoric times, giant animals—some of them two stories high—roamed the earth. There were huge camels and beavers the size of bears. In those days—from two million to 10,000 years ago—many animals were super-size! Even if the largest modern ELEPHANT weighed 22,000 pounds (10,000kg) and stood 13 feet (4m) at the shoulder, it was still only half the size of the Imperial Mammoth!

Now that the mammoths are gone, two kinds of elephants, the Asian and African, are the largest land animals. The African elephant is larger, with the world's biggest ears. But to tell the two types apart quickly, check out the trunk. Asian elephants have one lump on the end (called a lobe); African elephants have two.

Elephants have trunks for a very obvious reason. Their necks are too short to allow their mouths to reach the ground. Their trunk is an all-purpose tool that is used for just about everything: breathing, drawing up water for drinking, spray baths, maneuvering objects, greeting friends, hugging or spanking their offspring, even as a snorkel during deep-water crossings. But its most important use is gathering food.

WOULD YOU BELIEVE . . .

Elephants never stop growing during their entire 60-year lifespan, though they grow very slowly as adults. So the largest member of the herd is probably also the oldest.

Adult elephants can eat 330 pounds (150kg) of leaves, berries and twigs a day, all plucked with the trunk and placed in the mouth. Eating is very important to such large animals. They may wander 30 miles (48km) in one day searching for a good food source—often travelling down centuries-old paths called "elephant roads," worn down by generations of their ancestors. Once a suitable location is found, the day is spent in peaceful munching on tender leaves.

Plenty of food and a safe environment seems to make elephants happy, and like content kittens, they show their pleasure by purring. It's true—their tummies rumble with a sound that's a lot like a purr or low growl. The tummy rumbling noise carries for more than half a mile (1km) and serves to keep the elephants in touch with each other when they're in the dense brush. If one of them senses danger, its rumbling abruptly stops. The sudden silence warns the rest of the herd to be alert—kind of a reverse burglar alarm!

Thomas Kitchin, TOM STACK AND ASSOCIATES

ASIAN ELEPHANT *Elaphas maximus*

Larry Tackett, TOM STACK AND ASSOCIATES

CAPYBARA *Hydrochaeris hydrochaeris*

A MOUSE THE SIZE OF A HOUSE

. . . Dolls' house, that is. It's the South American CAPYBARA, at four feet (1.2m) long and 200 pounds (91kg), the world's largest rodent. "Chirping" along on partly webbed feet, the capy searches jungle-like areas around ponds for grasses, grains, water plants and fruit. Pretty quick on land, the capy runs just like a horse, but its first love is the water.

Water is a necessity for its good health (its skin is dry and gets sores without the moisture) as well as enjoyment. These rodents are as graceful as ballerinas in the water. They have "neutral buoyancy"—little or no weight in the water—and the slightest movement propels them across a pond.

Caimans (crocodilians) are the main enemy of the defenseless capy in the water. On land, avoiding jaguars and humans keeps the timid animal safe. Even though the capy isn't a threat to anyone, imagine your tame tabby's reaction to this giant mouse!

STEALTH, NOT SPEED

Would it surprise you to know that the shy, elusive LEOPARD is able to catch almost anything it feels like eating, from a tiny frog to an antelope larger than itself? Long considered Africa's cleverest hunters, leopards, are stalkers, not runners. They're also incredible jumpers—they can leap as high as a car length straight up and two luxury cars long! Quick as a wink, they're up in a tree, out of harm's way. This capable kitty, strong enough to lug a 50-pound (23kg) antelope dinner into the highest branches of a tree, is also smart enough to keep its kill away from other predators, such as lions and scavengers like hyenas.

Many leopards develop a taste for only one food—fish, for example. A leopard may live right next to a farm filled with all kinds of easy pickings, but never go near the farm animals, preferring to eat only its favorite food, even if it's much harder to come by. This partiality to a certain food may explain why some of the big cats became man-eaters!

AS AMAZING AS IT SOUNDS . . .

Sightseeing leopards raise their tails like a white flag, which lets other animals know they're not out hunting!

Jeff Foott, TOM STACK AND ASSOCIATES

LEOPARD *Panthera pardus*

Greg Vaughn, TOM STACK AND ASSOCIATES

CAMEL *Bactrian—Camelus ferus*

ONE HUMP OR TWO?

Did you know that CAMELS originated in North America? Fossil records prove it. They show the smallest to have been about the size of a rabbit and the largest a giant of 15 feet (4.5m) at the shoulder. As the creatures multiplied, a few crossed land bridges to other continents. Some went to South America, where they survive as llamas. Others went to Asia and became two-hump Bactrian camels. From those, another camel descended—the Arabian (dromedary) camel, which had only one hump. It survives as today's one-hump dromedary, a special domesticated breed. Both camels live in the desert of the Middle East and are used for riding, but the Bactrian has shorter legs and is more easy-going.

The camel's ability to go for long periods without water is legendary. But just how long is long? When they're not working, camels can endure up to three months without water! When working or walking in the heat of the desert, they can go about a week with absolutely no moisture—or several weeks if there are water-filled desert plants to snack on.

BELIEVE IT OR NOT . . .

There is no "normal" body temperature for a camel, just a normal range. It goes from 83° to 106°F (28° to 41°C) depending on the weather. Why? To avoid sweating away precious water on hot days!

Water is not stored in the camel's hump. The bumps on its back are solid fat, an energy reserve. To survive with little water, the camel uses the moisture stored in its tissues. It can loose up to 25 percent of its body weight and still do a good day's work. In comparison, if you weighed 100 pounds

Dominique Braud,TOM STACK AND ASSOCIATES

(45kg), you would be in big trouble if your weight dropped down to 75 pounds (33.75kg) from loss of water. Why? Because you would not only be losing moisture from your tissues, but also from your blood. Soon your blood would get thick and sticky and your heart would not be able to circulate it, and you'd be a goner. But take a look at the dehydrated camel, with its ribs sticking out and its skin hanging from its body. Ten minutes after that camel drinks 30 gallons (114 l) of water, it'll plump right up before your very eyes! Camels are the only animals in the world that can do this.

THE REALLY AMAZING PART . . .

A dried-out camel can lift the same 400-pound (182kg) pack and do the same work as a fully watered one!

WALK THIS WAY

In Central and South America, there is a creature that manages to walk gracefully and comfortably on its wrists! It's the ANTEATER, and its feet naturally turn under to protect the long claws it uses to rip open ant and termite hills—its favorite source of food.

You can guess from the anteater's very long nose that its sense of smell is good—40 times better than yours, as a matter of fact. It's good enough to sniff out the most hidden termite holes.

Surprisingly, in a face-off, the Giant Anteaster (3–4 feet/.9–1.2m) can usually fight off an attacker as powerful as a jaguar with its amazing coddled claws that are longer and sharper that those of a big cat! For the anteater, danger comes from above in the form of owls and hawks, its main enemies.

Walt Anderson, TOM STACK AND ASSOCIATES

GIANT ANTEATER *Myrecophaga tridactyla*

John Cancalosi, TOM STACK AND ASSOCIATES

BANDED ANTEATER *Myrmecobius fasciatus*

MARSUPIAL WITHOUT A POUCH

Yes, this little creature is an ANTEATER, too, even though it's only about the size of a squirrel. "Banded" refers to its beautiful striped coat. A native of Australia, it usually goes by its Aboriginal name "numbat." Though most marsupials have a pouch, numbats don't. To get a ride on their mother, the tiny babies must cling to her long stomach hair. When the mother decides that they're too heavy to carry around, she stores them temporarily in a ground-hole while she looks for food.

Numbats like to sleep in hollow logs and these are their main means of defense. After entering the log and tucking their tail under, they plug up the opening with their rear end, swelling themselves up to fit in tight as a cork. Pythons and goannas (big monitor lizards), their major enemies, can't get a grip on them to drag them out!

FABULOUS FACT . . .

The name for "stuffing the log" is "phragmoticism"!

Mary Clay, TOM STACK AND ASSOCIATES

SPINY ANTEATER (ECHIDNA) *Tachyglossus aculeatus*

NO ONE'S RELATIVE

This SPINY ANTEATER is no relation to either of the anteaters on the previous page. A native of Australia, it looks like a porcupine or hedgehog with a very long nose. But while it's a different species from the South American anteater, it has developed the same hunting equipment for catching the ants and termites it loves to eat: a long nose and a sticky eight-inch (20cm) long tongue. This is called "convergent evolution." It means that animals with different origins and ancestors end up with the same features because they live in similar conditions.

A monotreme, the spiny lays one single egg and carries it in a pouch. The amazing part is that the pouch does not exist until it is needed. Then the mother's flat belly muscles fold the stomach skin together to form a temporary egg-holder. After the baby hacks its way out of its shell, it stays in the holder for ten more weeks, lapping up the milk from the mother's pores. As soon as baby leaves, the pouch disappears, becoming ordinary stomach skin again!

WOULD YOU BELIEVE . . .

The numbat (page 13) is another example of convergent evolution. It's more closely related to the kangaroo than the spiny anteater!

WILL THE REAL UNICORN PLEASE STAND UP?

Did the unicorn ever exist? Well, we're pretty sure (aren't we) that it didn't, but if that's so, then where did the explorers find the prized unicorn horns that they brought back from their travels?

Let's look at the possibilities: Could the horn have come from the horned but ugly rhinoceros? No, that horn is too short. Or the male narwhal, a 16-foot (5m) member of the whale family, with its 8-foot (2.4m) long, twisted single tooth-tusk? No, too long and twisty.

DID YOU KNOW . . .

Treasured beyond gold because people believed it could neutralize poison, the unicorn horn was worth a king's ransom.

More likely the horn came from the Arabian ORYX, a pretty, smallish antelope-type of creature that is not often seen today but was once found throughout Arabia, Syria and Iraq. Unfortunately for the oryx, the horns were in such demand and the poachers so successful that the wild population became extinct in the early 1970s.

Bob McKeever, TOM STACK AND ASSOCIATES

ORYX *Oryx leucoryx*

Mark Newman, TOM STACK AND ASSOCIATES

ARCTIC GROUND SQUIRREL
Spermophilus undulatus

COPING WITH COLD

In the frozen wasteland of Alaska, the ARCTIC GROUND SQUIRREL sleeps nine months of the year. While the outside temperature is −50°F (−45°C), the squirrel's underground hideout is over 20°F (6.6°C), a full 70°F warmer! Safe from the killing cold, the little mammal practically suspends life for the winter. It goes into a very deep sleep. Its breathing slows; its bodily functions, such as heart rate and metabolism, slow down or stop altogether, and its body temperature drops to just above freezing. The hibernating squirrel only needs to use a little bit of energy to live through the winter on the fat stored in its body!

Those lazy nine months are going to cost it, though, because, when it does wake up, it only has three months left to do everything that it takes all year for a squirrel in a warmer climate to accomplish. Soon after waking, it mates and 25 days later its young is born. One month gone. The baby's eyes open three weeks after that, followed in three days by a search for roots and seeds. Now there's only one month left to grow, dig its own burrow and stock up on food for the coming nine-month hibernation. How does it do it? By working frantically at least 17 hours every day!

John Cancalosi, TOM STACK AND ASSOCIATES

HARRIS GROUND SQUIRREL *Ammospermophilus harrisii*

COPING WITH HEAT

The HARRIS GROUND SQUIRREL lives in the blistering heat of the deserts of the southwestern United States. The sand it walks on is sometimes 150°F (65°C). Its own body temperature goes up to 110°F (43°C). This hot-blooded rodent has a temperature every day, but it never gets sick! How does the squirrel do it?

For one thing, this squirrel doesn't lose any body water. In fact, even its urine is almost solid. When the heat gets to be too much, it dives down into its shady burrow. In the desert-burrow, the weather is cooler, because the soil insulates it from the heat aboveground. And if the fuzzy fellow has to go out, it can take an emergency measure and spread saliva all over its head to cool off. These cousins have really developed different ways to cope with the weather extremes they live in!

Joe McDonald, TOM STACK AND ASSOCIATES

CHEETAH *Acinonyx jubatus*

FASTER THAN A SPEEDING LOCOMOTIVE

No, not Superman, super CHEETAH! The fastest land animal is considered to be the hunting specialist of the short-grass plains. Usually unaggressive and mild-tempered, cheetahs need plenty of endurance to catch one of their favorite dinners—Thompson's gazelle. Called "tommies" for short, these gazelles are the most numerous animals in the plains community; herds of thousands of tommies bounce across the plain in an unusual gait known as "stotting," with legs stiff as a marionette's. Unfortunately for the tommies, they must also be quite tasty, because they are the prey of the jackal, hyena, Cape hunting dog and all the cats, including the cheetah, their biggest fan.

Cheetahs are built for speed, with their slim lithe

body, extra long legs and small head. They can sprint faster than most people drive—70 miles (113km) per hour—for short distances. They take advantage of these short bursts of fabulous speed with a specialized hunting technique. They approach the prey animal quite openly from afar, but always in profile, never head-on. Apparently, many animals do not regard the cheetah as a threat as long as it doesn't seem to be coming directly for them. When the crafty cat gets close enough, it quickly turns and charges, accelerating from 0 to 45 miles (72km) per hour in two seconds! Look out! But, it's too late for the tommie to escape!

Joe McDonald, TOM STACK AND ASSOCIATES

DID YOU KNOW . . .

Wild cheetahs only like fresh meat that they've killed themselves. They never return to snack on leftovers!

Measuring the speed of an animal in the wild is very difficult to do. That's why, in the 1920s, in London it was decided to *scientifically* race the cheetah against the greyhound. The race turned out to be inconclusive. Many suspected the cheetahs were more interested in eating the dogs than racing against them. A safe piece of advice might be: Don't bother racing a cheetah. You can't win and you could become dinner!

Nancy Adams, TOM STACK AND ASSOCIATES

SQUIRREL MONKEY *Saimiri sciureus*

MONKEY BUSINESS

If you think of apes as "first cousins" to humans, then MONKEYS would be second cousins. Apes, chimps and gorillas have a body structure that is closer to our own, with a generally heavier build, and a broad chest. Their organs, muscles and bones are also more suited to an upward stance. Monkeys, on the other hand (except for ground dwellers like baboons), usually have a longish, narrow body. Their organs are grouped like other four-footed animals. And, of course, monkeys have tails and apes don't. But maybe you've already guessed the most important difference. Apes far outrank monkeys in "brain power." More about apes later.

Monkeys are divided into two groups by geography. New World monkeys—the cebids and marmosets—live today in tropical Central and South America. Old World monkeys—langurs, baboons and others—live in Africa and Asia. Separated from each other for at least 30 million years, each group has developed its own way to cope with its environment.

IN FACT . . .

The most "sociable" award goes to the squirrel monkeys. They are always chattering.

Most striking is the "fifth hand," the "prehensile" tail of some of the New World monkeys. This fabulous tail is delicately ridged almost like a human finger and it can not only grasp a tree limb, but it also is capable of picking up a small peanut! Three out of six species have this feature: the cebus, the howler and the spider.

Another interesting feature: tough rump callouses, called ischial callosities, have developed in the Old World monkeys. These callouses allow the creature to sleep comfortably on a branch in a sitting position.

WOULD YOU BELIEVE . . .

A gibbon can touch its toes without bending over!

New World monkeys regularly have twins and triplets and the father is likely to take part in the child rearing. Old World monkeys usually have just one offspring and its mother will take care of it.

A simple way to tell New World and Old World monkeys apart is to look at their faces. A broad nose with well-separated, round nostrils that face outward—almost—belongs to a New World resident. A narrow nose with downward-pointing, comma-shaped nostrils belongs to an Old World monkey.

Kevin Schafer/Martha Hill, TOM STACK AND ASSOCIATES

MANDRILL *Mandrillus sphinx*

DID YOU KNOW . . .

Mandrills are the most brilliantly colored baboons. Their faces flush even more intensely just before a fight. Sometimes that's enough to scare the enemy away.

WOULD YOU BELIEVE . . .

A legend from South African bushmen claims that baboons can talk. But they never let men hear them for fear of being put to work!

BEST OF BOTH WORLDS

BABOONS are some of the largest Old World monkeys (see page 21). Males can reach 100 pounds (45kg), females half of that. Baboons take advantage of the best of both primate worlds. They don't live exclusively in trees (like most monkeys) or on the ground (like most apes). They search the ground for easy-to-find food during the day and escape the reach of predators by sleeping in the trees at night.

Baboons live in big families called troops. The arrangement of a troop moving across the open grassland is very specific. Smaller males walk to the front and rear; older dominant males cover the sides; females and youngsters travel within this caravan, and at the center come the mothers and babies. If any monkey spies danger, it gives a sharp bark. A male troop member will immediately move away from the group to watch the intruder. If the intruder makes the slightest move, a double bark sounds the alarm. All the youngsters run for their mothers; the females carrying infants escape first, then the juveniles, the females and finally the small males. The dominant males are likely to turn and stand their ground. They are very brave and actually capable of fighting off a leopard!

MAY I BORROW YOUR COMB?

Wouldn't it be great never to lose your comb? The SLOW LORIS doesn't ever have that problem—because its comb is in its mouth! Its evenly spaced teeth get rid of tangles, while under the loris' tongue is a feather-like kind of finger called a sublingua that removes the bits of fur that get stuck in this dental comb!

INCIDENTALLY . . .

Being slow also makes sneaking up on your dinner easier. Surprisingly, the loris is able to grab its prey with amazing speed!

The loris is about the size of a house cat with the shape of a monkey (it's related), and covered with soft, fluffy hair. And this hair is very important, because the loris has such a slow rate of **metabolism** that losing its hair—even in the tropics, where it lives—would mean dying of the cold!

So how does such a slowpoke escape from the snakes, cats and birds that want it for lunch? Apparently, pretty well! When startled, the loris simply lets go of the tree branch it's hanging from and falls out of reach. It's risky, but the only means of a quick exit for the loris.

Rod Planck, TOM STACK AND ASSOCIATES

SLOW LORIS *Nycticebus coucang*

DID YOU KNOW . . .

Getting bitten by the sweet-looking loris can be risky for humans. Its toxic saliva can cause a severe allergic reaction—even death!

G.C. Kelley, TOM STACK AND ASSOCIATES

OTTER *Lontra canadensis*

Nancy Adams, TOM STACK AND ASSOCIATES

YOU WOULDN'T KNOW A MONSTER IF YOU SAW ONE

You've heard of the Loch Ness Monster and maybe you've seen pictures of it—you know, sea-serpents drawn with a head and a line of humps following? There are supposed to be lots of these lake monsters. Well, they may be easier to explain than you think! The long sleek OTTER naturally swims showing three humps: the head, back and tail. After their mothers give them their first nudge into the water, the young otters swim with her every day, following her lead in a perfect line of little humps. Sometimes two families swim together. When the mother in the lead lifts her head to see "What's happening?" Bingo! There are the head and humps of the monster!

Otters like the cold water. Some of them even hang out around Arctic ice! They're comfortable because of the 800 million fur fibres that trap warm air next to their body. These fibres are so dense that water never touches their skin.

Otters don't hibernate. They keep fishing even when the lake is iced over, diving down and coming up to breathe through holes in the ice. If there aren't any convenient breathing holes, they come right up under the ice and breathe out. This creates an air-bubble that loses carbon dioxide into the ice and water. The oxygen trapped in the ice rushes in to take place of the carbon dioxide. The otters then inhale the oxygen that is now in the bubble and go about their business!

CAN'T CATCH ME!

Zooming across the desert at a blistering 35 miles (56km) per hour, the BLACKTAIL JACKRABBIT zig-zags like a professional football player. Usually, it outruns its enemies, but if that doesn't work, it flashes a quick change, turning its body towards the enemy very slightly, so that its hair appears to change color from its normal tan to white. This ability is called "directive coloration," and it confuses the pursuer long enough for the rabbit to escape.

Hares also count on speeding to safety. Their favorite trick is called "jinking." Just when it looks as if they're about to be caught, they turn sharply to the left or right at full speed, sending the hunter racing straight ahead after empty space. Watch the hare's ears! The hare always flattens its ears against its head just before jinking.

DO YOU KNOW . . .

How rabbits are different from hares? In addition to being a little smaller, true rabbits give birth to many naked, blind young in underground nests. Baby hares are born above-ground in the open, one or two at at a time, with a full coat of hair, working eyes—and in less than five minutes they are able to run!

Wendy Shattil/Bob Rozinski, TOM STACK AND ASSOCIATES

BLACKTAIL JACKRABBIT *Lepus californius*

THE FURRIEST ANIMALS

In the cruel environment of northern Canada, Alaska and Greenland, where the temperature hovers at a breathtaking −50°F (−45°C), and storms frequently drop that by another mind-boggling 20°F, survives the animal that the Arctic natives call *oomingmak*, or "bearded one." Very distant relatives of wild cattle, MUSK OXEN look like sloppy water buffaloes. The "big bruisers" are the furriest animals alive! They have a six-inch (15.25cm) thick layer of dense, wooly hair called "quiviut," and guard-hairs so long that they brush the ground. This extraordinary coat helped their ancestors survive the Ice Age, and is even protection from Eskimo arrows.

AS A MATTER OF FACT . . .

Musk oxen are so well insulated that when they lie down, the snow does not melt under their bodies!

Today musk oxen are protected from humans by the Canadian government. The only thing they need to fear is hungry wolves. No problem. Musk oxen stick together when the wolves start to prowl, forming a tight ring—a "circle-the-wagon" maneuver—with their tail ends to the inside and their sharp horns pointed out towards the enemy. The young are safely sheltered in the center as the big guys make lightning-quick strikes at the wolves, trying to gore them. This strategy holds off even the most determined wolf!

Brian Parker, TOM STACK AND ASSOCIATES

MUSK OXEN *Ovibos moschatus*

John Cancalosi, TOM STACK AND ASSOCIATES

RATS *Rattus villosissimus*

RATS!

Since the first man climbed on a raft, seamen have been plagued by RATS. As stowaways on every oceangoing vessel, these resourceful, fuzzy creatures have also been the ultimate carriers of death. It was tiny fleas living in the fur of rats that spread the Black Death, a plague that killed half the people in Europe during the Middle Ages. But the rats managed to stay alive! Like the other animals you're reading about in this book, they have many strategies for survival.

For example, on the other side of the world in the Pacific Ocean are hundreds of surface-level coral islands and reefs that are next to impossible to see from the deck of a ship. Naturally, before radar, ships often ran aground and were destroyed. A scientist spending the night on a barren (that means no trees, no name, no nothing) coral island, couldn't figure out how the hundreds of shipwrecked rats living there had managed to stay alive! No food, you see. Then one day he discovered the rats fishing, or more correctly, crabbing! These clever rodents would sit on the rocks with their tails dangling in the shallow water, waiting for a crab to foolishly take the "tail bait." The rats got fed, the crabs—well, never mind about that part.

DIGGING THE DIRT

The one and only member of the order *Tubulidentata*—the AARDVARK—lives only in Africa. The most unusual and specialized of the termite-eaters has a remarkable talent—it's a spectacular digger! Aardvarks can dig out a four-foot (1.2m) long burrow faster than a team of six men digging furiously with shovels. The aardvark's powerful claws make it easy for it to get into the rock-hard termite mounds to devour its favorite dinner. Its tough, bristly nose skin—and the dense nose hairs that close off its nostrils during digging—keep the aardvark safe from termite bites, while its 18-inch (45cm) long tongue scoops up the insects—ants in the dry season, termites when it's wet. The surface of the aardvark's teeth is like no other mammal's. There's no enamel on them; instead they are covered with a substance called cementum, which is usually found on the roots of other animal's teeth. Cementum is made of mineral salts and water, and is about as hard as bone.

WOULD YOU BELIEVE . . .

Aardvarks sometimes smell like rotten fruit, which is lucky for them because that smell attracts their favorite dinner—insects!

AARDVARK *Orycteropis afer*

Gary Milburn, TOM STACK AND ASSOCIATES

Brian Parker, TOM STACK AND ASSOCIATES

DOLPHIN *Delphinus delphis*

GOOD SAMARITAN OF THE SEA

Dolphins are mammals that long ago renounced their land-dwelling ways and returned to the sea. They are actually small whales that can swim better than some fish. The flippers that guide them through the water are all that remain of what were once front limbs. Traces of bony skeleton indicating long-gone legs are now covered by a sleek swimmer's body. And though air is what they breathe, they spend 98 percent of their time underwater.

Even though you can't see their ears, dolphins have super hearing. Their use of **sonar** was discovered by accident during World War II. Arthur McBride, head of the world's first dolphinarium, in Florida, was trying to catch a bottle-nosed dolphin in murky water without success when he realized that the dolphins were making very rapid clicking sounds as they swam at breakneck speed towards the waiting net traps. Then, at the last minute, they veered off. The dolphins "knew" the nets were there without being able to see them! Dolphins use this ability—called **echolocation**—as a kind of supersense, to avoid running into danger, to locate food, even to communicate. Here's how it works: The dolphin sends out whistles or clicks at the rate of 20 to 800 per second (far beyond what humans can hear). The speed and the way the sound bounces off an object and returns to the dolphin gives the animal a wealth of information about the objects nearby—their size, speed, shape, direction, and whether they're food or non-food.

Brian Parker, TOM STACK AND ASSOCIATES

Communication is very important to this species that depends on cooperation for gathering food. A small group of dolphins may start a "fish roundup" by swimming 30 feet (9m) apart, herding the prey towards the surface. They take turns breaching—jumping out of the water and slapping back in—stunning the fish and causing them to panic. From as far as six miles (10km) away, other dolphins will hear the activity and join in. Twenty or 30 individuals may grow to an efficient fish-catching group of 300 dolphins working together.

Dolphins not only communicate and work together, they help others. In November 1993, a dwarf pygmy whale was spotted heading for Tigertail Beach, Marco Island, Florida. Accompanying it were two dolphins, one on each side of the floundering and obviously ill whale. Witnesses insist the dolphins were helping the whale by holding the sick animal upright on its way to beach itself on the shore. They stayed with the sick whale until it got all the way up onto the sand. Then they headed back out to sea.

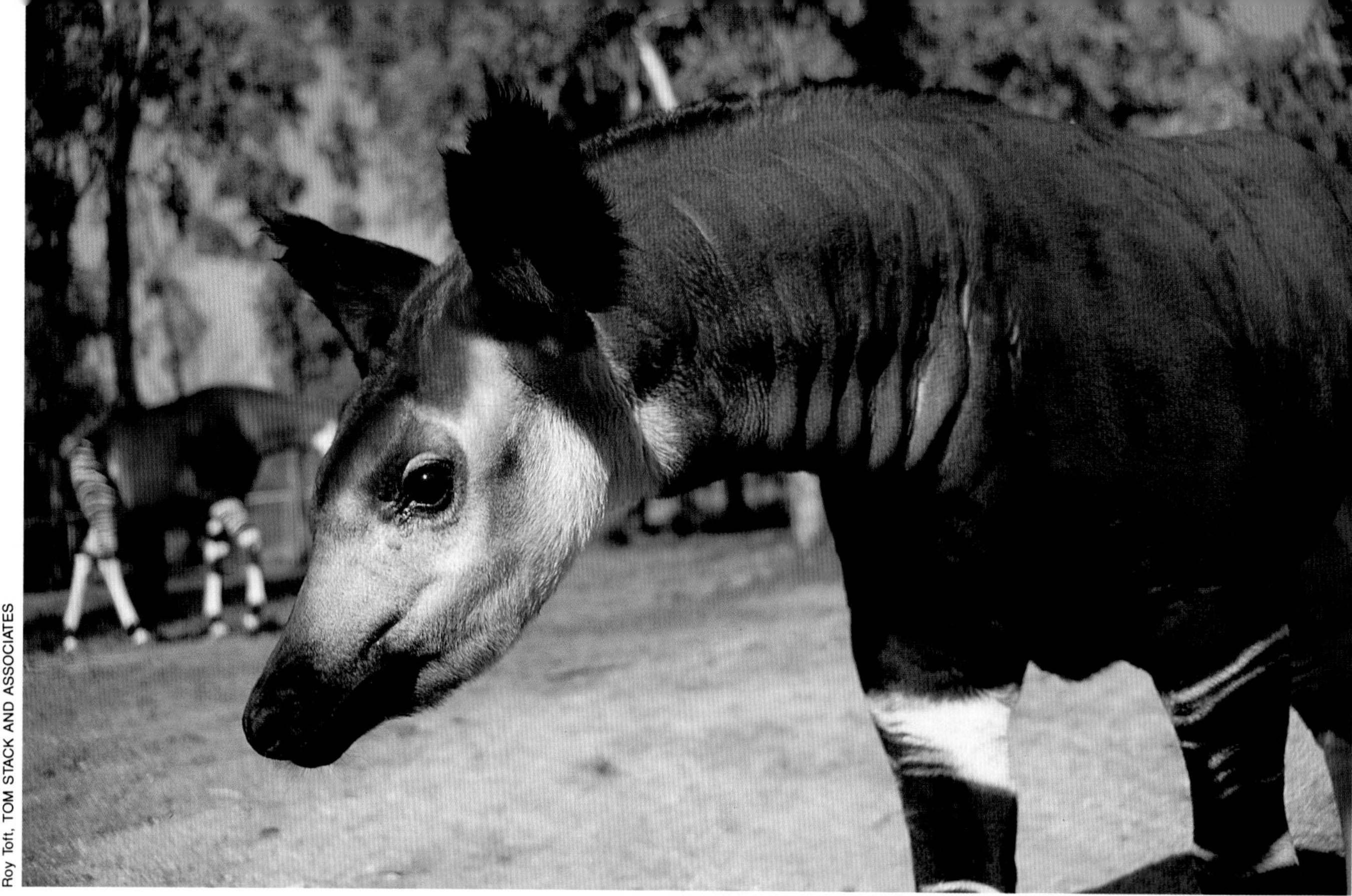

Roy Toft, TOM STACK AND ASSOCIATES

OKAPI *Okapie johnstoni*

AN ANIMAL WITH A 4-PART STOMACH

It's not surprising that a secretive animal from the dense rainforests of the eastern Congo was one of the last large mammals to be discovered (1900). The solitary OKAPI is the giraffe's only living relative. Although the okapi is much smaller (only about as tall as a man), its body shape is similar to a giraffe's and it was thought at first to be a cross between a giraffe and a zebra!

Okapis, along with cows, camels and many other mammals that have hooves instead of claws, are called ungulates. Many of them also chew a "cud." Scientists refer to them as ruminants. All ruminants are plant-eaters. Plants are great sources of carbohydrates (sugars and starches), but usually very low in protein, which is a must for growth and cell repair. This means that the okapi must utilize every bit of protein in the plants it eats. Nature has solved this problem by developing a complex digestive system for the ruminants, which is like no other. It is designed to break down the tough plant fibres that would otherwise be indigestible.

DID YOU KNOW . . .

Okapis' tongues are black, giraffes' blue!

This is how it works: When the animal takes a bite of food, it doesn't bother chewing too much and quickly swallows it into the first stomach (rumen). After digesting for a while and, when the okapi isn't busy eating new food, the stomach contents are returned to the animal's mouth to be chewed at leisure (this is the "cud"). Finally, the food goes on to *three* additional stomachs where microorganisms process and reprocess it until every nutrient possible is extracted and used! Of course, it takes a long time—almost four days—to completely digest one meal! But don't get the idea that okapis eat only once every four days. New food is eaten all the time. The stomach can tell the difference between digested and undigested food and moves it along the "digestion track" at the right time!

Roy Toft, TOM STACK AND ASSOCIATES

INCREDIBLY . . .

The okapi neck is very flexible, able to move every-which-way. Combine that with an extremely long tongue and you've got an animal that can lick itself anywhere and everywhere!

WORLD'S TALLEST ANIMAL

From the point of view of the tallest animal in the world, the GIRAFFE, the okapi is a midget. Look at it this way: Your dad can stand eyeball to eyeball with the okapi, but it would take your mother on your dad's shoulders, plus your sister standing on your mother's shoulders and you on top of the acrobatic tower to see eye-to-eye with the tree-topping giraffe!

DID YOU KNOW . . .

Giraffes live in the tree-dotted grasslands south of the Sahara Desert in Africa.

It's hard to believe that those long necks have the same number of vertebrae as ours—seven. Each vertebra is drawn out to a length of eight inches (20cm) or more! As holder of the "World's Tallest Animal" record, giraffes use their height and keen eyesight to keep tabs on each other from as far away as a mile (1.6km). You can tell a male from a female giraffe from quite a distance by the way it eats. Females bend their heads down over their meal of leaves and twigs, while the males stretch up to their full height, trying to reach the highest new shoots. This curious habit reduces the chance of competition between the sexes.

Giraffe mothers usually give birth at the same

Barbara von Hoffmann, TOM STACK AND ASSOCIATES

GIRAFFE *Giraffa camelopardalis*

HARD TO BELIEVE, BUT . . .

Adult giraffes sleep little, if at all—about a half hour in every 24, in 5-minute catnaps!

"birthing grounds," probably where they themselves were born. Although their disposition is pretty "laid back," they're very protective of the 12 calves that will be born to them in their lifetime, and always on the lookout for any lion foolish enough to try to run off with a baby. Their heavy soup-plate-size hooves can easily bash in the skull of the biggest cat!

Giraffes appear neat and clean, because, unlike other huge animals such as the elephant and rhinoceros, they don't go in for mudbaths. What they do like is a bite of salty-tasting dirt, now and then, because it contains minerals their body needs.

AMAZINGLY . . .

Startled giraffes can gallop 30 miles (48km) per hour for short distances.

Brian Parker, TOM STACK AND ASSOCIATES

Mary Clay, TOM STACK AND ASSOCIATES

WESTERN CHIPMUNK *Tamius minimus*

SAVED FOR A RAINY DAY

We all know that some rodents gather food to save for the time of year when no food is available. We call this behavior "hoarding." People do it all the time (go look in your closet). but the first-place hoarding award absolutely goes to the CHIPMUNK. Up to a bushel of nuts (that's enough space for 30 litres, eight gallons or 128 eight-ounce glasses of milk!) may be stored in its main burrow, just where you'd expect to find them—under the bed! It's true! Chipmunks prefer to sleep *on* their stash! And that's not all. This industrious storer has small emergency stashes hidden all over its territory. Sometimes it forgets just where it left some of the buried nuts. But that's part of a clever plot by Mother Nature. In the spring the forgotten seeds will germinate and new trees will grow, providing a continuing food source for our furry friend.

THE TRUTH IS . . .

Chipmunks and squirrels don't "remember" where they bury nuts, but they can smell them—even under a foot of snow!

Gary Milburn, TOM STACK AND ASSOCIATES

SHORT-TAILED SHREW *Blarina brevicauda*

SURPRISING SHREWS

Dolphins (pages 30–31) and bats aren't the only animals that use *echolocation* for communication—so does the SHORT-TAILED SHREW! And not only that! For their size (4–7 inches/10–19cm long), these small, fuzzy ancestors of the first true mammals may also be the fiercest creatures on earth! And this is despite the fact that they are born blind, deaf, without hair or teeth and some no bigger than a peanut.

BY THE WAY . . .

If you should ever come upon a shrew, don't pick it up. There are only a few venomous mammals and this is one of them!

ON THE OTHER HAND . . .

Not all shrews are poisonous, but how will you know the difference?

The "Atlas" of the shrew clan is the four-inch (10cm)—four more inches are tail—HERO SHREW. This tiny animal can support a medium-sized man on its back! How does it keep from getting squished? The hero shrew's arched backbone is the most unusual in the animal kingdom. It is several times thicker and stronger than the shrew's other bones, and the backbones of other shrews. Its strength comes from its extra width and from ridges that lock one vertebra to the next. What use is this feature to the shrew? Only Mother Nature knows for sure!

John Shaw, TOM STACK AND ASSOCIATES

CARIBOU *Rangifer terandus*

KEEPING WARM

The North American CARIBOU are the larger, wild version of Europe's reindeer. They roam the frozen Canadian plains, coming together in herds of thousands to make the annual migration to summer feeding grounds. They often stop along the way to paw a hole in the snow, hoping to get at their favorite meal, a lichen that grows in the far north called "Caribou moss." Lucky for the caribou, there's no competition for this sparse food. Its acid content makes other animals sick. Not the caribou, which thrives on 12 pounds (5.4kg) of the quick-burning, carbohydrate-rich moss every day. This heat-producing food-fuel keeps the caribou's body temperature at a comfortable 105°F (40.55°C).

To prevent heat loss, those long skinny legs have a temperature that is 50°F (27°C) cooler than the body!

Just as your clothes keep you warm, the caribou's hair keeps it warm. The club-shaped hair is thicker at the outside tips than at the base, forming a thick outer layer that traps tiny warm-air spaces close to the skin, with a fine curly underwool. The coat is so warm that the caribou seems completely unaffected by the cold weather.

BY THE WAY . . .

A caribou will never be able to sneak up on you. Its ankles click when it walks!

To make the treacherous migration over slippery ice and snow, its large feet work like snowshoes. The two halves of the cloven hooves are flattened out, which reduces their pressure on the ground to two pounds (.9kg) per square inch, a very light weight. An animal of similar size, the moose, which doesn't have flattened feet, exerts eight pounds (3.6kg) per square inch. Without their big feet, the 700-pound (318kg) caribou would sink like a rock in the soft snow!

Thomas Kitchin, TOM STACK AND ASSOCIATES

Thomas Kitchin, TOM STACK AND ASSOCIATES

HIPPOPOTAMUS *Hippopotamus amphibus*

MANNERS MATTER

Some animals have what certainly look like "rules of social behavior" that the whole group respects and abides by. Consider the HIPPOPOTAMUS: The Greeks called it the River Horse, and with good reason. The huge muscled creature likes to spend most of the day in the water, floating and snoozing, sometimes submerging for a half hour. Actually, it has to stay wet. The water keeps its delicate skin from burning. The hippo's unique skin structure allows water to evaporate five times faster than it does on our skin. To protect itself, the mighty mammal even has its own built-in suntan lotion, a pink substance produced by glands under the skin that prevents the burning ultraviolet rays from getting through. This fluid is so red that many natives insist the hippo "sweats blood"!

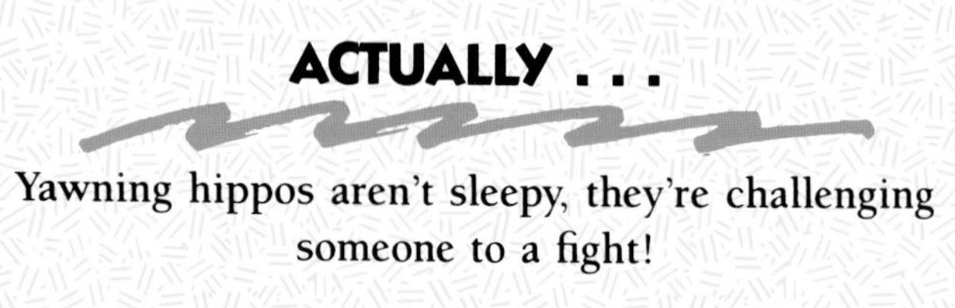

Groups of 20 to 100 hippos live together. The children and females stay in a central area called a "crèche." This is close to but separate from the adult males, each of whom has his own separate "refuge." When it's breeding season, the female chooses her mate by entering his refuge. A male may visit a female too, but only with her approval. When he enters the female area, the male must be calm and never aggressive. If one of the females gets up, he must lie down and not get up until she lies down again. Failure to follow the "rules" will result in the male being attacked by all the females.

AS A MATTER OF FACT . . .

Mother hippos are even happy to "spell" each other by babysitting!

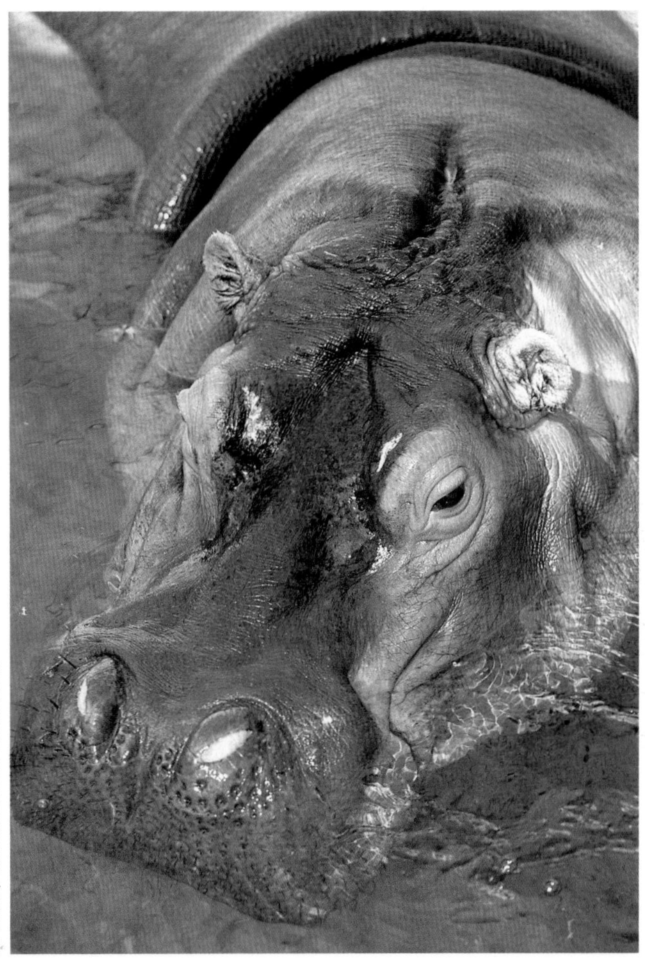

Bill Everitt, TOM STACK AND ASSOCIATES

Hippo society is ruled by the females and the males abide by their wishes. Hippo mothers teach their young the "rules" of good hippo manners, including how to follow instructions and pay respect to their elders. When walking, the youngster must remain exactly at its mother's shoulder. If she starts to run, so must baby. If she stops, baby stops. She teaches her youngster everything it needs to know to get along in the hippo world!

Dave Watts, TOM STACK AND ASSOCIATES

GREY KANGAROO *Macropus giganteus*

DID YOU KNOW . . .

To be called a kangaroo, the animal's feet must be longer than 10 inches (25cm). Wallabies' feet are shorter!

BOOMERS AND FLYERS

The world's largest marsupial—the GREY KANGAROO—can grow to 8 feet (2.4m) tall and weigh over 200 pounds (91kg). On most continents, deer, antelope, goats and horses eat grass and vegetation that grows on the open plains. In Australia's vast, arid interior, the kangaroo has taken the place of these familiar four-hoofed grazing animals. It spends the day sheltering from the sun's heat and the night peacefully feeding. The kangaroo's biggest problem isn't animal predators, it's the human race. Not only do people kill kangaroos but they also brought the sheep to Australia (it's not a native species) that compete for the same grass! Fortunately for the "boomers" (male kangeroos; females are called "flyers"), their digestive systems are very efficient. A part of the kangaroo's stomach uses bacterial action to break down the hard-to-digest plant cellulose that it eats. So, even though the kangaroo is much larger than the sheep, it only has to eat about the same amount to produce a far superior result—kangaroos are 52 percent muscle, sheep only 27 percent. During the dry season, when food and water are in short supply, kangaroos use their strong front limbs to dig for and create water holes that many different animals use—even where no surface water is visible.

Kangaroos frequently have to travel long distances to get a meal, and here's where the animals' amazing speed comes in handy! Kangaroos travel in great leaps of up to 27 feet (8.2m) long and 10 feet

BELIEVE IT OR NOT . . .

Nervous kangaroos lick their forearms!

(3m) high, at 20 miles (32km) per hour for distances, with bursts of 55 (88km)! While hopping may look like an awkward means of movement, it's much more energy-efficient than four-legged running. The kangaroo's strong leg muscles and huge feet are the power behind the jump and how it gets its family name, *Macropodidae* (*macropus* means big feet). The large tail acts like a counterbalance at landing. As you can imagine, those big feet also make formidable weapons! They're not only gigantic, but equipped with a sharp claw that can be used to lash out and down in one of the most powerful blows that can be delivered by any mammal! The usually docile kangaroo can quickly kick almost any enemy to death with those fantastic feet!

NOT SURPRISINGLY . . .

Only the males get into fights. The flyer saves herself for motherhood!

Dave Watts, TOM STACK AND ASSOCIATES

CONVEYER BELT TEETH

Looking like small (2–3 feet/.6–.9m tall), very furry kangaroos, the ROCK WALLABIES of Australia are also marsupials. Like all marsupials, their babies are born after a very short time and finish developing in their mother's pouch. They're called "Joeys." The little rock wallaby is different from all its relatives. For one thing, it's only half their size, but the most important difference is its teeth. When you lost your baby teeth, another tooth was waiting below each one, ready to push right up through the gum and fill the empty space. The little wallaby's nine molars stand in a row waiting for the forward one to get worn down. When it falls out, the next in line moves forward to take its place. Only two other mammals have teeth like this—the elephant and the manatee!

BELIEVE IT OR NOT . . .

Some burrowing marsupials (wombats and koalas) have upside-down pouches. This is a convenient arrangement because it means that dirt and rocks don't get inside!

ROCK WALLABY *Petrogale inornata*

John Cancalosi, TOM STACK AND ASSOCIATES

Spencer Swanger, TOM STACK AND ASSOCIATES

LION *Panthera leo*

FAMILY PRIDE

LIONS are the only sociable wild cats. Their families are known as "prides" and are usually made up of 20 to 30 animals. One dominant male, several lesser males and many females and cubs cooperate in the chores of hunting and defending the pride.

Even though lions can run 40 miles (64km) per hour for short periods, jump up one story and leap over four car lengths, they usually don't climb trees like many of the other cats do. Lions rely on surprise, cunning, silence and, most of all, teamwork, for a successful hunt. They are master strategists, seeming to confer with one another to devise a successful plan.

For example, let's say the pride has spotted a small group of wildebeests and carefully positioned the main ambush group downwind, hidden in the grass. Two smaller groups of lions break off and circle around in opposite directions. coming up to the side and behind the wildebeests. Their plan is to drive the prey straight into the jaws of the waiting ambush party! It works—and dinner is served!

Jeff Foott, TOM STACK AND ASSOCIATES

POLAR BEAR *Thalarctos maritimus*

HOW COLD IS COLD?

To avoid the intense Arctic cold—as low as −70°F (−55°C) with a 30-mile (48km) per hour wind—most animals hibernate or migrate. Yet, one of the largest carnivores, as well as the largest of the bears, does neither. POLAR BEARS choose to live on the permanently frozen landscape year round. Scientists estimate that about 15,000 polar bears roam the 5 million square miles (13,000,000 sq km) of land around the North Pole. That's not really many bears, only one for every 333 square miles (866 sq km). In some areas, the local people, called Inuits, claim that they have never seen the "wandering one" (polar bear). They call it the *pihoqahiaq*.

WOULD YOU BELIEVE . . .

Seals in the Antarctic are much calmer than their Arctic cousins, probably because there are no polar bears at the South Pole!

How does this amazing animal cope with the incredibly cold weather? For starters, the bear is warm-blooded. In other words, its internal thermostat keeps its body temperature at a steady 100.8F (38.22C), but that's not the only thing. Its body shape is designed to retain warmth. It is rounded and compact—no big ears or long tails (big heat losers). And since large objects lose heat more slowly than small ones, the bear, which can weigh up to 1,600 pounds (726kg), stays warmer longer!

Jeff Foott, TOM STACK AND ASSOCIATES

To maintain its size and all those layers of fat, the polar bear often eats 100 pounds (45kg) of its favorite food, seal blubber, at one sitting. Half of the food it eats is used to keep up its body temperature (same as for humans). The colder it gets, the more food the animal needs to keep warm. Naturally, polar bears eat lots!

AMAZING BUT TRUE . . .

Polar bears can smell a dead meal 20 miles away and a live seal three feet (1m) under the ice!

AND BESIDES THAT . . .

Legends claim that the white bear covers its black nose with its paw when stalking prey!

Polar bears don't mind jumping into the icy water after food. In fact, they're tireless swimmers, frequently seen dog-paddling at six miles (10km) per hour. They've occasionally been found as far as 50 miles (80.5km) out at sea! Fat and two layers of dense, oily fur (very complex, with a hollow core) help them stay afloat.

IF IT'S MONDAY IT MUST BE WASHDAY

Have you ever watched the industrious RACCOON as it cleverly manipulates pieces of food with its oh-so-agile fingers (right up there with the chimpanzee!)? This "masked" mammal was originally named *Ursus lotor*, or the "washing bear," because of its reputation for washing its food before eating it. People who have watched claim they've never seen a wild raccoon wash its food. Scientists finally discovered that what the raccoons were really doing was dunking and then retrieving the food—it only looked like washing. Animal food got dipped more often than plant food. Strangely enough, the dirtiest food—earthworms—got dunked the least! But the animals in the study were in captivity, where all food comes from the land—and from a human provider. In the wild, the raccoon's food usually comes from the water—fish, snails, things like that. So eventually the experimenters realized that the raccoons were acting out catching water-food, *not* washing land-food. Your tame tabby will do the same thing if you give it a toy mouse. It will pounce on the pretend prey, throwing it around, imitating a real hunt!

Brian Parker, TOM STACK AND ASSOCIATES

RACCOON *Procyon lotor*

IT'S TRUE THAT . . .

As you go north the raccoons get larger!

DON'T LET THE BLOOD GO TO YOUR HEAD

Probably one of the most bizarre mammals alive today is the South American TWO-TOED SLOTH. Sloths spend nearly all day—and all night, since they're really nocturnal—hanging upside down. Time to eat—upside down. Sleep—upside down. Mate, have a baby, feed the kid—all upside down! They use their long curved claws like hooks, to hang from. Because of these claws, they can't walk or even stand on their feet! Don't they get a headache looking at everything upside down? No need to worry—the sloth can turn its head 270°, so it can actually look at you right-side up if it feels like it. This turned-over tree dweller blends right in with the rainforest foliage. Algae growing along its hair strands tints the sloth—green in rainy weather, yellow during drought. From the ground this slow-moving creature with a *spurt* speed of 10 feet (3m) a minute seems almost motionless and it looks like just a bunch of leaves to a hungry jaguar!

BY THE WAY . . .

Two-toed sloths really have three toes on their back feet.

YOU NEVER GUESSED . . .

Three kinds of moths, certain beetles and many mites call the sloth's colorful fur home!

Gary Milburn, TOM STACK AND ASSOCIATES

TWO-TOED SLOTH *Choloepus didactylus*

SUPER SKIN!

Who's 3,500 pounds (1,589kg), five feet (2.2m) tall and a vegetarian? You guessed it—it's the rhino, of course! Rhinos are pachyderms (that means "thick skin"), just like elephants, and some legends even claim that their hides are bulletproof! Of course, that isn't true, even though an approaching rhino does look as unstoppable as an armor-plated tank! You'd have to be awfully nearsighted not to notice a rhino if it charged at you, but scientists wonder whether the rhino, with its little-piggy eyes set far to the sides of the head, actually sees *you*! In other words, no one is sure if the rhino is charging because it *does* see you or because it *doesn't* and is simply running towards an unusual sound! Of course, if you get run down, it probably doesn't really matter.

WOULD YOU BELIEVE . . .

The rhino's horn is not like the elephant's tusk. It's made of glued-together hair.

BLACK RHINO *Diceros bicornis*

Joe McDonald, TOM STACK AND ASSOCIATES

Bill Everitt, TOM STACK AND ASSOCIATES

RINGTAIL or CACOMISTLE *Bassariscus astutus*

SECRET SUNBATHERS

Many animals are shy and do their best to stay away from humans. Naturally, many of them do their roaming around at night. We call them "nocturnal." Animals that are active during the day are called "diurnal." But even night-roaming creatures seem to like the sun. This 2½-foot (.8m) long relative of the raccoon called the RINGTAIL or CACOMISTLE (Mexican for "bush cat") loves to come out for a sunbath. You won't see the ringtale; it does its basking in the very tops of the trees, stretching out fully along a branch, as if lying on a chaise longue!

Manfred Gottschalk, TOM STACK AND ASSOCIATES

LLAMA *Llama quanicoe*

BUILT FOR THE HEIGHTS

The South American LLAMA (pronounced "yama") is a great example of "adaptive radiation." It has the same ancestors as the camel, which lives on the other side of the world, and similar characteristics, such as the split lip, long, curved neck and lack of skin between thigh and body. But after three million years of separation, it has adapted to a totally different environment. While the camel lives in the low-altitude heat of the desert, the llama lives in the cool mountains, at heights up to 13,000 feet (3,965m).

The llama is especially well equipped for dealing with the oxygen-poor atmosphere of the mountains. It never gets light-headed in the thin air. That's because its red blood corpuscles are unique among mammals. They are elliptical (egg shaped), and are able to take in more oxygen and live longer—235 days compared to 100 days for human red blood corpuscles—than the usual round cell. The ability to utilize all available oxygen is very important to a high-altitude dweller!

John Cancalosi, TOM STACK AND ASSOCIATES

NINE-BANDED ARMADILLO *Dasypus novemcinctus*

A REAL LIVE TANK

The largest armadillo is the three-foot (.9m), 130-pound (59kg) ARMADILLO of eastern South America. It got its name from the Spanish word *armado*, which means "one that is armed." Most of the armor in animals is made of hair that is pressed together, like the horn of the rhinoceros. But not the armadillo! Its protection is made of small bony plates, each one covered by a layer of hard skin. This walking tank is covered from head to tail with these plates that form a turtle-shell shape. Only its tummy is bare. If a threatening bird or animal shows up, the armadillo pulls its legs in and wedges itself down firmly on the ground—or rolls up in a tight ball—secure in its suit of armor.

DID YOU KNOW . . .

The nine-banded armadillo can submerge in water for six minutes!

Dave Watts, TOM STACK AND ASSOCIATES

PLATYPUS *Ornithorhynchus anatinus*

STRANGEST CREATURE ON EARTH

There are only two kinds of egg-laying mammals in the world (monotremes) and the PLATYPUS is one of them (the other is the spiny anteater—page 14). Early visitors to Australia could not believe their eyes when they saw this odd-looking creature. Here was a water-dwelling, burrowing, warm-blooded, furry creature that gave milk but laid eggs and dredged up dinner with a duck-like bill. At a loss for a name, they simply called it a "duckbill."

Dave Watts, TOM STACK AND ASSOCIATES

ODD BUT TRUE . . .

No fossil monotremes have ever been found!

Platypus ancestors have been around for over 135 million years, virtually unchanged! It seems that when Mother Nature created the duckbill she put some of her favorite animal structures together in a whole new way. Take the duck-like bill, for example: Its resemblance to a bird's beak is only skin deep. The platypus' dark grey bill is a moist, nerve-filled tool used to search muddy river bottoms for shrimp, worms and crayfish. It can sense the tiny electrical impulses given off by all living things, and this is a big help in finding its prey. When it resurfaces after a couple of minutes, its cheek pouches will be stuffed. Eventually, the platypus will eat the equivalent of 1,300 worms a day, while floating on the surface.

The platypus' front feet are webbed like an otter's, but the webbing extends beyond the end of the toes, creating a large paddle that can be pulled back, leaving the claws free for digging.

The strangest feature is the rattlesnake type of curved fang, called a poison spur (though with a less deadly venom), that is attached to the male's back legs. The spurs are used for defense, not for hunting. Sounds unbelievable, doesn't it!

A flat, muscular tail like that of a beaver brings up the end and is used as a swimming stabilizer and quick-dive assistant.

Now, imagine all this covered with fur (except the bill and webs)! Amazing.

Nancy Adams, TOM STACK AND ASSOCIATES

GORILLA *Gorilla gorilla*

TERROR OF THE TREETOPS

Not so! The giant GORILLA, as tall as a man and three times as heavy, eats only greens. His caveman display, pounding his chest, roaring, rearing up and throwing whatever's handy—usually just plants—is all show! Natives claim that gorillas will not attack a man who stands his ground, only those who turn and run away.

DID YOU KNOW . . .

Gorillas sleep in "nests" ten feet (3m) off the ground, curled up in the manner of humans!

Gorillas have an unusual animal "phobia." They're afraid of water! The mighty mammals are reluctant to cross the smallest streams. In the wild they don't even drink, preferring to get their moisture from their food—fruits and plants. The closest a gorilla willingly gets to water is soaking the fur on the back of its hand and sucking the water off!

HARD TO BELIEVE, BUT . . .

You'll know a gorilla is really mad when it sticks its tongue out at you!

Larry Brock, TOM STACK AND ASSOCIATES

PACK RAT *Neotoma micropus*

NUTS TURNED TO GOLD

Can't find your favorite marble? Don't blame it on your kid brother—blame it on the PACK RAT. It looks like a big hamster about the length of your arm, though one-third of that is tail. These rodents like to live in the dry parts of North America. They also like to hoard "things"—especially bright, shiny or colored things—and frequently filch anything that catches their eye and is small enough to carry! But, in their way, they're honest souls, usually leaving something behind in exchange.

One day some lucky miners discovered that the local pack rats had made off with a container's worth of shiny metal nuts, one by one, only to replace them with dull unprocessed gold nuggets! Now, that's a good deal!

What do the rats do with their treasures? Just like people, they build homes with "rooms" to house their possessions.

Brian Parker, TOM STACK AND ASSOCIATES

KOALA *Phasolarctos cinereus*

IT'S A DANGEROUS WORLD

A living "teddy bear" and Australia's most beloved tree-dweller, the KOALA is usually a toy-sized two feet (.6m) tall and 33 pounds (15kg), covered by thick, soft, grey fur. It seldom ventures to the ground, and when it does, it's only to eat a bite of dirt (helps in digestion) or to scamper from one tree to another. The koala probably took to the trees in pursuit of its favorite and only food—the leaves of the eucalyptus tree, also called gum or tallow.

The koala's food fetish is specialization carried to a dangerous degree! Eucalyptus only grows in a slim slice of eastern Australia—the most heavily populated by humans—so that is where the koala must live. Out of the hundreds of varieties of eucalyptus, the koala eats only 12. Of these 12, each koala prefers five and has a single favorite. Add to this the fact that at certain times of the year food trees produce an overabundance of prussic acid, a deadly poison (¼ of a pound/.11kg would kill a sheep)! Fortunately, the poison builds up in different trees at different times.

At night, koalas climb to the top of the trees to eat the tender new shoots. If there aren't enough new shoots to make up the koala's 2¼-pound (1kg) daily requirement, they have to eat tough, older leaves with strong-smelling oils that are hard to digest. The good news is that these oils act like bug repellant, so koalas are lice- and vermin-free. The bad news is that koalas smell like super-strong cough drops!

BY THE WAY . . .

Koalas have a dozen names, among them: bangaroo, koolewong, karbor, narnagoon and most interestingly, New Holland sloth!

Life for the koala is a constant gamble. Because of its very limited diet, its survival could be in grave danger. If anything should happen to the eucalyptus trees, koalas might simply vanish from the face of the earth!

Brian Parker, TOM STACK AND ASSOCIATES

Joe McDonald, TOM STACK AND ASSOCIATES

RHINOCEROS VIPER *Bitis nasicornis*

REALLY RADICAL REPTILES & AMPHIBIANS

BELL'S
HORNED FROG
Ceratophrys ornata

Gary Milburn, TOM STACK AND ASSOCIATES

GREEN CRESTED BASILISK *Basiliscus plumifrons*

REP-TILE Cold-blooded vertebrate that breathes air and usually has a skin covering of scales or bony plates.

AM-PHIB-I-AN Cold-blooded vertebrate with smooth, scaleless skin, that starts out life in the water as a gill-breathing tadpole. Later, it usually develops lungs and limbs, and spends part of its time on land.

Reptiles (4 orders)	**Amphibians (3 orders)**
Turtles	Frogs and toads
Crocodilians	Salamanders and newts
Snakes and lizards	Caecilians (worm-like creatures)
Tuatura	

The study of reptiles and amphibians is called **herpetology**, from the Greek word *herpo*, which means to creep or crawl.

WHAT DOES IT MEAN TO BE COLD-BLOODED?

Scientists call reptiles and amphibians "**ecto-therms**," *ecto* meaning "out" and *therma* meaning "heat"—without heat or *cold-blooded*. But what does that mean?

Most mammals have higher body temperatures than reptiles. To maintain that high body temperature, mammals use half (or more) of the food that they eat to generate body heat. They are warm-blooded **(endotherms)**.

Reptiles don't waste food-energy on producing heat. They absorb heat and cold directly from their surroundings. This doesn't mean that they are at the complete mercy of the elements. Reptiles use what scientists call **behavioral temperature control**—seeking out or avoiding sunlight as needed. After a cool night, snakes and lizards bask in the sun to restore a high enough temperature to go on with the business of living—that is, eating and mating.

Because they have gotten around the heat problem, cold-blooded creatures need much less food to survive. This explains why reptiles live so successfully in food-scarce areas—like the desert! If conditions get really bad, amphibians and reptiles can just "shut down," hibernating until the problem of no food or cold weather simply passes.

NOW YOU KNOW WHY . . .

Some reptiles eat only three or four times a year!

Of course, even though reptiles can be found almost everywhere—except in the polar regions—the majority live in tropical and semi-tropical parts of the world.

But, strangely enough, while cold may be a problem for reptiles, heat is worse! Although most lizards can withstand body temperatures up to 107°F (42°C), anything higher could be fatal. Desert dwellers are careful to be active only in cooler periods of the day. At noon they find protection in the shade or by burrowing down into cooler sand. Some reptiles avoid the problem altogether by hunting at night!

KEEP IN MIND . . .

As you learn more fascinating facts about these unusual creatures, always remember that more than any other animals the reptiles' simplest everyday activity is always affected by the weather!

Brian Parker, TOM STACK AND ASSOCIATES

AMERICAN CROCODILE *Crocodylus acutus*

IT'S THE WAY OF THE WORLD

The world that we live in is 4.6 *thousand million* years old, a constantly changing place where extinction is the rule and existence the amazing exception! When the ancestors of early amphibians and reptiles inched their way from the warm ancient seas 365 million years ago they faced an incredible challenge—survival! Evolution is all about survival and that's why creatures change, grow and reproduce.

Here's how it works: Some animals possess a trait that makes it easier to get along. Perhaps they're larger, quicker, have sharper teeth or longer claws, or eat food that no one else wants. They have a much better chance of living than their brothers. Maybe they can even live long enough to pass the valuable characteristic on to their offspring! The tiniest change may take millions of years, but, with luck, the adaptation finally becomes normal for the species.

Whenever their surroundings change—become hotter, drier, colder—animals must change, too! The early reptiles were so successful at adaptation that they expanded into 16 orders of every size, shape and description. Then the environment changed, and thousands of species of dinosaurs and other animals could not adapt quickly enough to avoid extinction. When the "ruling reptiles" vanished a mere 65 million years ago, the less "significant" mammals found themselves with a whole world to expand into—and they did!

Brian Parker, TOM STACK AND ASSOCIATES

PTERODACTYL *Pterodactylus*

NECESSITY IS THE MOTHER OF INVENTION

Pterosaurs are a group of extinct flying reptiles and that is just what their name means, "flying lizard." The first fossil pterosaur ever found was named PTERODACTYL (it lived 160–65 million years ago). Pterodactyls are classed as reptiles, but scientists believe that they were warm-blooded with a covering of fur! They took to the air on leathery wings stretched between finger bones, featuring claws at the mid-point. The long snout resembled a bird's beak, but was filled with tiny teeth, and the bones were hollow and light enough for the animal to get airborne. To achieve the vision and coordination required to fly, Pterodactyls had to have a much larger brain than other reptiles of the same size.

The photograph here is of a scientific reconstruction based on the fossilized bones of Pterodactylus.

WOULD YOU BELIEVE . . .

John Cancalosi, TOM STACK AND ASSOCIATES

GLASS SNAKE *Ophisaurus ventralis*

The AUSTRALIAN TREE DRAGON has a tail four times its own length!

At night the ALLIGATOR's eyes glow rosy-pink, a great aid to poachers. The cause is reflected "rhodopsin"—the chemical that makes night vision possible!

When a 120-pound person closes his mouth, the jaw pressure is around 60 pounds, but when a 120-pound CROCODILE does the same, the pressure rises slightly—to 1,500 pounds! Imagine getting bitten by that!

GLASS SNAKES are very stiff, because each scale contains a little bone called an "osteoderm." Thank goodness they have a groove running down the side or they'd be too stiff to move!

AND BESIDES THAT, DID YOU KNOW . . .

GATOR tails can propel the alligator's whole body vertically out of the water!

DWARF PUFF ADDERS (snakes) retreat into the sand tail first!

Most crocs are slow and awkward on land, but JOHNSTON'S CROCODILE (Australia) is capable of a full gallop, like a horse!

ANACONDAS, PYTHONS and BOAS have left-over tiny hind legs. They no longer use them to get around, but they can move them!

A green covering of fuzzy algae disguises the CHINESE SWAMP SNAKE from the small fish it eats!

The fastest snakes alive, BLACK MAMBAS, cruise at 7 miles (11km) per hour, and have a sprint speed of 15 miles (24km) per hour!

Some TREE FROGS shed their skin every evening!

RED-EYED TREE FROG *Agalychnis callidryas*

D. Barker, TOM STACK AND ASSOCIATES

Manfred Gottschalk, TOM STACK AND ASSOCIATES

KOMODO DRAGON *Varanus komodoensis*

A DRAGON LIVES!

The KOMODO DRAGON lives—you guessed it!—on Komodo, an island near Indonesia. It's a tough place to get to and the komodo's last protected habitat.

BY THE WAY . . .

It's not a good idea to get bitten by the komodo. It has a bacteria in its saliva that will probably kill you if its teeth don't!

This huge monitor lizard has a nasty disposition and the size to back it up! In fact, with the full-grown length of a luxury car (12 feet/3.7m) and a weight of 380 pounds (136kg), it is the largest living lizard! It's easy to see how these dragons can, and do, snack on young goats, deer or even people foolish enough to get too close!

That's how the Sultan of the neighboring island of Sumbawa kept his subjects in line. Criminals and other "undesirables" were deported to the uninhabited Komodo, where the ferocious creature, with its keen tracking skills and knife-like claws, would hunt down its unlucky prey.

THE DEVIL'S FROG

What would you do if a fat 10-inch (25.4cm) long frog suddenly jumped out at you! What if it looked like a green devil with horns sticking out of the top of its head, right above the eyes? Well, what you'd better do is jump back! You've just been hopped by the South American AMAZONIAN HORNED FROG, a beautifully colored creature with a very mean streak! It's big on biting fingers and hangs on more like a bulldog than a bullfrog. This fearsome character thinks nothing of eating its brother, which in an odd way is good. At least, this gruesome activity controls the frog's numbers.

ONCE UPON A TIME . . .

The Argentinians, famous for raising beautiful horses, have claimed (wrongly) that the bite of a horned frog, on the lip of a grazing horse, would kill it (the horse, of course!).

AMAZONIAN HORNED FROG *Ceratophrys cornutas*

D. Barker, TOM STACK AND ASSOCIATES

Ed Robinson, TOM STACK AND ASSOCIATES

GIANT LAND TORTOISE *Geochelone elephantopus*

DID YOU KNOW . . .

Land tortoises can be found all over the world—in Europe, Africa, Asia and all of the Americas, even on isolated islands like the Galapagos—but not in Australia!

THE UNDISPUTED CHAMPION

TORTOISES have always been thought to be slow, but they're really not that poky. Some of them can crank up to two miles (3.2km) per hour. That's nearly as fast as you can walk. Not bad, considering that it's lugging a huge shell on its back! The tortoise's specialty is its shell, and that tough armor, modified by nature to suit every environment, has ensured its survival for 175 million years. The bulky shell doesn't come off—it's part of the living animal. The top plate (called the *carapace*) is firmly attached to the backbone and the belly is covered with a piece called the *plastron*. They are joined together at the side by a bony bridge.

BESIDES THAT . . .

The largest land tortoise in the world—51 inches (130cm) shell length—is the Aldabra. It lives in the Seychelles, a group of islands in the Indian Ocean.

Tortoises are also extraordinary because they live longer than any other animal. Reports of 150 years are common! Imagine the famous giant "Tonga Tortoise" that was presented to the ruler of Tonga by the explorer Captain James Cook in 1774. The tortoise was already quite old, but it went on to live through the Revolutionary War, the Civil War, World Wars I and II, the Korean War and Vietnam, not to mention the invention of just about everything we take for granted. This aged tortoise was blind in one eye, had survived two brush fires, being trampled by a horse and run over by a cart! It's believed to be well over 200, but its age can't be confirmed, because all the records on Tonga are oral, not written!

Jack Stein Grove, TOM STACK AND ASSOCIATES

HARD TO BELIEVE, BUT . . .

Tortoises are in danger from hyenas. They can bite completely through the tough shell!

Ed Robinson, TOM STACK AND ASSOCIATES

John Gerlach, TOM STACK AND ASSOCIATES

CHUCKWALLA *Sauromalus obesus*

TAIL OF A LIZARD

Poor lizards! Snakes, birds, mammals, and even bigger lizards—just about everyone preys on them! The lizard called the CHUCKWALLA has an unusual means of dealing with persecution! It doesn't just run away. When it is pursued, it squeezes into the nearest rock crevice, wedging itself in by blowing its body up to half again its normal size. Its scales catch on the rock, making it almost impossible for the hungry enemy to pull it out. If worse comes to worst, as a last resort the chuckwalla does that old lizard favorite—losing its tail—in hopes of being left alone. How does it do that? There's a weak spot in every lizard's tail, sort of like a perforation, where the muscles and blood vessels can come apart neatly and there is very little bleeding at the separation. Obviously, if someone grabs a lizard's tail, it will come off easily at that spot, but lizards have another strategy: If they're taken by the neck, they'll shake their own tail off! When this happens, the tail continues to wiggle and move off in another direction. That often confuses the enemy enough to make it drop the real lizard and go after the tail!

DID YOU KNOW . . .

Scientists call the ability to cast off an unneeded body part "autotomy."

Lizards think twice before dumping their tails. Although the tail grows back and can be dropped off time and time again, it will never get back the original markings, lost vertebrae or specialized tail functions—locomotion, grasping, displaying and social standing too (it may have less opportunity to breed because of its less-than-handsome tail). But, most important of all, many lizard tails store the fat necessary for winter survival, and that can be a tragic loss in a cold climate!

AS A MATTER OF FACT . . .

Autotomy is common in invertebrates, such as lobsters and insects, but not often seen in creatures with a backbone. Most lizards but only a few others (some rodents and salamanders) have mastered this trick!

Rod Planck, TOM STACK AND ASSOCIATES

D. Barker, TOM STACK AND ASSOCIATES

ALLIGATOR SNAPPING TURTLE
Macroclemys temminckii

LURED FOR LUNCH

Whoops! No finger! That's what you'll be saying if you're weird enough to stick your hand in the mouth of the North American ALLIGATOR SNAPPING TURTLE, one of the largest freshwater turtles in the world. This turtle likes a bite of meat and what kind doesn't much matter. Witness the clever way it gets its dinner. The Snapper lies perfectly still down in the mud on the bottom of the pond. It opens its toothless, beak-type mouth and waves a small reddish, worm-like stalk, attached to its tongue, as a "lure." Sooner or later, a small fish is sure to come close to investigate what looks to him like a meal. Then, quick as a wink, the turtle has caught its dinner!

WOULD YOU BELIEVE . . .

Turtles weren't always toothless; some ancient fossil finds had teeth!

ACTUALLY . . .

Leatherback turtles at 3,000 pounds (1,361kg) are the largest living turtles!

Joe McDonald, TOM STACK AND ASSOCIATES

Mary Clay, TOM STACK AND ASSOCIATES

SOLOMON ISLAND SKINK *Corucia zebrata*

SAND SWIMMERS

What is it? It's spotted, striped, banded or a solid color. It may have legs and it may not. It's a lizard that's called a SKINK! The Solomon Islands' two-foot (.6m) long Giant Skink even has a prehensile tail—a tail like a monkey's that can be used to grasp things. And that is just what it needs for climbing trees and hanging on to branches.

Another skink, the Five-Lined Skink, has a beautiful shiny blue tail when it is young. Its unusual color supposedly attracts predators, but when they grab it, the skink plays an old lizard trick and just lets the tail drop off—it's disposable! This trick that draws the attention to a disposable part is called "deflective coloration"—and it enables the skink to escape from many a dangerous situation.

Skinks are found all over the warmer parts of the world. Some even live in the desert, burying their eggs as deep as six feet (1.8m) underground. They get that deep by wiggling their sleek bodies, "swimming" through the sand.

AS A MATTER OF FACT . . .

Skinks can breathe underground because the loose, dry sand they "swim" in lets some air through.

David M. Dennis, TOM STACK AND ASSOCIATES

COBRA *Naja naja*

SURPRISINGLY . . .

Very few elephants die from snake bite, but some do—from cobras!

CHARMING SNAKES

Most of us would agree that the COBRA, growing to eight feet (2.4m) or so, is one impressive snake! How brave, or foolhardy, is the snake charmer, swaying rhythmically back and forth with his flute, mesmerizing the snake with the lilting music—*hold it!* Snakes are deaf! That's right, scientists say they have no eardrums, and therefore they can't hear airborne vibrations. If that's so, what is fascinating the snake? The clever snake-charmer keeps his pets inside a dark basket. When the lid is suddenly lifted, the surprised and half-blinded snake rears up in its typical hood-spread, defensive position and fixes on the first moving object it sees—the flute. The snake is not moving with the beat of the music; it's following the motion of the object!

WOULD YOU BELIEVE . . .

At one time cobras were thought to be able to "hypnotize" anyone who looked in their eyes!

Spitting cobras have developed the habit of shooting venom at people or animals that they feel threatened by. Accurate up to 9 feet (2.7m)—they're aiming for the victim's eyes, where the poison is sure to cause pain and temporary (sometimes permanent) blindness. Victims must be tied up to keep from scratching their eyes, which would allow the poison to enter their bloodstream, causing pa-

Robert C. Simpson, TOM STACK AND ASSOCIATES

MONGOOSE *Helogale parvula*

ralysis and death from suffocation. Staring into the eyes of a cobra is certainly intimidating. Rudyard Kipling tells the story of how the mongoose Rikki-Tikki-Tavi confronts and saves its human family from a pair of cobras. The mongoose avoids the snake's "hypnotic" stare and triumphs by employing bravery, wit and a common mongoose trait—endurance! By quickly jumping back and forth the mongoose keeps the snake on constant alert. The venomous viper finally becomes so tired that it's no longer able to hold its head up in striking position. Then the mongoose jumps the cobra!

AS A MATTER OF FACT . . .

The King Cobra is the largest venomous snake in the world at 16 feet (5m), with a head as large as a man's hand—and it's also the most intelligent!

Joe McDonald, TOM STACK AND ASSOCIATES

BULLFROG *Rana catesbeiana*

WHEN IS A FROG NOT A FROG?

Frogs do two things extremely well. They catch insects and avoid birds! That's why they've been around for many millions of years! Of all the animal groups in the world, frogs are the least harmful to humans. Too bad we can't say the same!

BY THE WAY . . .

The greatest leaper of all is *Rana fascinata,* an African frog that hops 14 feet (4.2m)!

Many animals are born little (and not so little) duplicates of their parents. Amphibians are an exception, and the BULLFROG is a good example. When its 25,000 half-inch eggs float on the surface of the water, encased in their cocoon of jelly, and start to hatch, what comes out are **larvae** that don't look anything like frogs! The frogs' children look like fish! They have flattened tails for swimming, eyes on the sides of their heads and they even breathe through gills!

It could take days, months or even years before the amphibian larva starts to look like its parents. The process is called **metamorphosis**, and the cooler the weather, the longer it takes. In northern climates it takes bullfrog **tadpoles** two years to look like froglets! Here's what happens: First the tail shrinks, as the food stored there is used up by the growing larvae. Then the back legs with their tiny webbed feet pop out on either side of the retracting tail. Soon the right front and finally the left front legs appear. The eyes move from the sides of the head to their prominent, bulging spot on the top. The gills shrink and lungs grow, and the digestive system changes in preparation for the adult's **carnivorous** lifestyle. Tadpoles prefer plants, but the eight-inch-long adult bullfrogs have enormous appetites and eat just about anything that moves, including insects, worms, crayfish, small terrapins and alligators, garter and coral snakes and, believe it or not, an occasional mouse or bird! Before you know it, one of nature's most amazing transformations has taken place and a tiny tadpole has become a full-grown frog!

CAN YOU IMAGINE . . .

Some frogs can retract their huge bulging eyes back into the roof of their mouth to aid in swallowing!

Joe McDonald, TOM STACK AND ASSOCIATES

BROWN ANOLE *Anolis sagrei*

YOUR EMOTIONS ARE SHOWING

Like the Old World chameleons, ANOLES use camouflage to hide, changing from green to brown and shades in between, depending upon whether they're sitting on a leaf or tree bark. Anoles also turn brown when the weather is cool (under 70°F/17°C) and bright green on warm sunny days. Surprisingly, the lizard's mood plays a part, too. The loser of an anole argument shows negative emotion by turning brown; the winner remains green, an "up" color!

How does this happen? The **hormone** "intermedin" is responsible. It is produced in the pituitary gland, near the part of the anole's brain that controls emotion. The bloodstream races the hormone to special color cells, causing changes in the pigment.

INTERESTING . . .

The anole has many devices for attracting a mate. One of them is displaying an otherwise hidden, brightly colored flap of skin called a "dewlap." You can see it in this picture.

PRIMITIVE BIOLOGICAL WARFARE

The French explorers of the Caribbean island of Martinique were met by a most inhospitable host. They named it FER DE LANCE, because of its lance-shaped head and body. Perhaps you've guessed that I'm talking about a snake, a **pit viper**, one very poisonous slitherer! The fer de lance is a classic "ambush" predator, sometimes hiding by a mammal trail for weeks until an unfortunate meal happens by! Like all pit vipers, the fer de lance has small depressions, or "pits," on its face between the eye and the nostril. The many nerve endings in the facial pits are so sensitive to the tiniest changes in temperature that they can detect the heat left from a warm-blooded animal that passed over the ground 20 minutes before! If the snake chooses to pursue dinner, a "scent trail" may be picked up by its perceptive tongue!

AS A MATTER OF FACT . . .

Other explorers also met up with the fer de lance. The Spanish called it *barba amarilla*, meaning "yellow beard"!

FER DE LANCE *Bothrops atrox*

Kevin Bohaper, TOM STACK AND ASSOCIATES

John Cancalosi, TOM STACK AND ASSOCIATES

TUATARA *Sphenodon punctatus*

THE THIRD EYE

The very last holdout of an ancient group of reptiles that are even older than the dinosaurs, the TUATARA has survived for over 200 million years, with only minor changes in its skeleton, while all the rest of its order Rhynchocephalia have died off. The so-called "beakheaded" reptiles live today in a nature preserve on Stephen's Island and on other small islands off the coast of New Zealand.

At first glance, the tuatara looks just like an ordinary two-foot (.61cm) long lizard, but no—it clearly is not. At least, not to scientists. Tuataras have no external ears as lizards do, and if you cut one open you could see hook-like extensions on its ribs—a bird-like feature. In the top-center of its head is a third eye, covered by a thin layer of skin. All the parts are there, the retina, lens, nerve endings, everything except the muscles. The eye is not used for seeing, and scientists now believe it may be used as a homing device, allowing the animal to judge where it is in relation to the sun.

Tuataras are remarkable for their very low rate of **metabolism**. Normally, they take one breath every seven seconds but, if need be, they can go for an hour without breathing! The islands they live on are not tropical, and tuataras are still active at 52°F (11°C), the lowest recorded temperature for any reptile activity! No wonder they flourished during the Age of Reptiles!

Tuataras are also one of the longest-lived animals. A full-grown two-pound (.9kg) male may be over 100 years old! They won't mate until they're over 20 years old, and even then the eggs won't be laid for a year after fertilization and they take another 15 months to hatch—much, much longer than any other reptile's.

John Cancalosi, TOM STACK AND ASSOCIATES

THE TRUTH IS . . .

When tuatara eggs get too cold, development stops. That's why they take so long to hatch!

Tuataras regularly share nesting burrows with sea birds, digging petrels or shearwaters, but there's no problem with overcrowding! The bird goes off fishing during the day and the tuatara goes out feeding at night. When the tuatara hibernates, the bird migrates. It's a perfect arrangement, except that the tuatara has been known to dine on bird eggs!

CAN YOU IMAGINE . . .

Tuataras have *two* rows of teeth on the top, and the single bottom row fits right in between!

Dave B. Fleetham, TOM STACK AND ASSOCIATES

BANDED SEA SNAKE *Hydrophis cyanocinctus*

SERPENT STOMACH PROBLEMS

For any fish—including sharks—foolish enough to chow-down on the BANDED SEA SNAKE, the results can be disastrous. It's not what you think. Big fish don't have to worry about the venomous sea snake from the *outside* because it can't bite through the tough fish scales. But many fish swallow their dinner in one piece, so the whole snake gets swallowed into the unwary diner's stomach and the irritated snake takes a nip! The snake's deadly venom rushes into the fish's bloodstream, and that's the end of the fish. But it might not be the end of the sea snake! The dying victim may vomit it up and the snake could get the last laugh, as it swims away!

NEVER TRUST A SNAKE

Most SEA SNAKES hang out in relatively shallow water feeding on the fish and their eggs that gather around coral reefs. But some adventurous sea snakes spend their days floating across the open ocean, going wherever the wind or current takes them! It looks as if these snakes are "sitting ducks," but they're not. Many have vividly colored skin to warn predators that they are quite poisonous!

DID YOU KNOW . . .

In some sea snakes, the lung runs almost the entire length of the snake!

ON THE OTHER HAND . . .

Some sea snakes return to land to mate, and all lay their eggs on land. Reptile eggs can't be laid in water—they'll drown!

Floating sea snakes don't have to search for food. They have their own larder cruising right along with them. You see, small fish tend to gather under any floating object—dead or alive—and soon "adopt" the snake, swimming around its tail (they're too smart to get near its head!). When the snake wants a meal, it begins to swim *backwards*, tricking the fish into thinking that its head is its tail! **ZAP!** Dinner is served!

INDONESIAN SEA SNAKE *Naen manado*

Mike Severns, TOM STACK AND ASSOCIATES

Bob McKeever, TOM STACK AND ASSOCIATES

SIDEWINDER *Crotalus cerastes*

SNAKY MOVES

Lizards developed before snakes, and so did lizard-locomotion! To move ahead, the lizard puts its right front leg forward and its back left foot forward, then vice versa. The result of this action is a wiggle—the forerunner of legless motion. In fact, lizards and snakes are so closely related that they are in the same group—*Squamata*. Some lizards have even lost their legs (worm lizards), while some snakes (like an anaconda) have the remains of lost limbs! Snakes have gone on to perfect living without legs, and have developed four ways of getting around:

Rectilinear locomotion: This is simply moving straight ahead by "walking" on its skin. The broad, flat belly scales on parts of its body slide forward, catching the ground like tractor treads and pulling the rest of the body along (the snake has to have loose skin for this to work). Often used on smooth surfaces, this subtle movement allows heavy snakes, like boas and vipers, to sneak up on prey.

Lateral undulation: This is the familiar snaky motion. The snake uses the irregular surface of the ground to help it move, getting a hold on rocks, twigs, whatever, and pushing against them.

Concertina locomotion: The snake's head stretches outward, uncoiling the tight double-S shape of its body. It gets a "neck hold" and pulls the rest of its body forward into a coiled shape again.

Sidewinding: This interesting movement is great for skimming across the desert's soft sand. There's even a snake named for it—the SIDEWINDER. The snake's S-coiled body turns sideways to go forward. Only two parts of the sidewinder's body touch the hot sand at any one time, leaving behind very distinctive diagonal-ladder marks in the sand.

WOULD YOU BELIEVE . . .

When a sidewinder is cold, it can turn its body a darker hue so it absorbs more heat!

Kerry T. Givens, TOM STACK AND ASSOCIATES

DART POISON FROG *Dendrobates azureus*

A DEATH-DEALING FROG

Imagine a poison so powerful that a drop will kill a person! Called batrachotoxin by scientists, this lethal liquid is produced by the tiny, one-inch (2.5cm) long, KOKOI FROG of Colombia, South America. Dart Poison Frog (its common name) doesn't bite; it doesn't have to. Its poison comes through the pores in its skin. One beautifully colored jumper supplied the native Indians of western Colombia with enough toxin to prepare 50 blow-gun darts by rubbing the tip over the back of the living frog! The big question is, who gets to catch the frogs, especially since even holding one in your hand could be enough to do you in!

DID YOU KNOW . . .

The bright colors of most dart poison frogs warn would-be predators to stay away!

GROWING UP IN A FLOWER

You can see why one of the most fabulously colored of the dart-poison frogs is named STRAWBERRY DART FROG.

This rain-forest frog takes care of her babies in her own way. She doesn't use the frogs' usual watery pond to incubate them—instead, she lays them on the damp leaf-litter of the forest floor. Now and then she comes by to urinate on them to keep them moist! The hatching larvae have the usual fish-like tadpole shape, but nowhere to swim! What now?

The female Strawberry Dart encourages one tadpole to wriggle onto her back where her sticky **mucus**-covered skin keeps it in place. As quick and agile as can be, she hop-climbs high into the forest trees looking for an **epiphytic** plant, such as a **bromeliad**. Epiphytes are plants that attach themselves to trees or other plants for support, but get their food and water from the air. Their thick, waxy leaves form a cup that collects rainwater. Into that "baby-bath" steps the mother frog. When the mucus holding the piggybacker in place dissolves, the tiny tadpole is safely swimming in its own nursery pool! Each tadpole is carried to its own plant and left, along with an unfertilized egg for food. The mother delivers more food every few days and before you know it, the young frogs hop down to the forest floor to begin their adult bug-eating days!

STRAWBERRY DART FROG *Dendrobates pumilio*

D. Barker, TOM STACK AND ASSOCIATES

Nancy Adams, TOM STACK AND ASSOCIATES

GHARIAL *Gavialis gangeticus*

THE RULING REPTILES

Just by looking, you can see that CROCODILIANS are a living bridge back to the Age of Dinosaurs. In fact, crocs and dinosaurs were both members of the same group of reptiles, the "archosaurs," or "ruling reptiles." The name certainly fits: Crocodilians are the largest, smartest and most advanced of all their kin. Once there were 108 species of crocodilians. Now there are only 23, in three families:

Alligatoridae = alligators and caimans
Crocodylidae = crocodiles
Gavialidae = gharials

The easiest way to tell the three groups apart is to look at their heads. Alligators have wide, flat heads. Their noses are rounded and from the side all you can see are the upper teeth—the lower ones fit inside the mouth.

The triangular, pointy snout belongs to the crocodile; you can see its teeth, top and bottom, on the outside.

No one could mistake the gharial's oddly shaped nose. It's very long and thin with a bulb on the end, and its hundred pointy teeth are all the same size.

HARD TO BELIEVE, BUT . . .

The crocodilians' larger back legs indicate that their ancestors may have once walked upright!

EL LAGARTO—THE LIZARD

El lagarto is what the exploring Spaniards called the thousands of ALLIGATORS decorating the river banks of the New World. Alligators are one of only a few crocodilians that live well outside the tropics. There are two species: One, the Chinese Alligator, is only found in the lower Yangtze River valley of eastern China and is very rare. The other lives in the southern part of the United States.

Amazingly, the sex of alligator babies is determined by the temperature in the nest. This is called **TSD (temperature-dependent sex determination)**. Eggs incubated at 90–93°F (32–34°C) are males, and those kept at temperatures of 82–86°F (28–30°C) are females; 87–89°F (30.5–31.6°C) produces equal numbers of males and females. The sun hitting the top of the nest makes it the hottest—boys; the bottom is coolest—girls!

WOULD YOU BELIEVE . . .

Some turtles lay their eggs in the gator's nest—when she's not looking, of course! And it doesn't seem to bother the gator!

AMERICAN ALLIGATOR *Alligator mississippiensis*

Joe McDonald, TOM STACK AND ASSOCIATES

CROCS ON THE NILE

The Greeks first met up with CROCODILES while travelling in Egypt 2,000 years ago. The huge Nile River crocs reminded them of the tiny wall lizards in their homeland called "Krocodeilos." And that's how it happened that one of the largest living reptiles got its name from one of the smallest.

Many crocodiles dig their nests in the sand, and, like the alligator, the heat in the nest determines the sex of the babies. But in this case, the hottest eggs produce girls. Could TDS (temperature-dependent sex determination) partially explain the amazingly quick and total disappearance of the dinosaurs 65 million years ago? What if TDS applied to dinosaur eggs too? Then the cooling (or heating) of the earth, whatever caused it—a meteor, a natural disaster or climate changes—could have produced all boys or all girls. And that would have been that!

SURPRISINGLY . . .

Even some creatures that live in saltwater need to drink fresh water. Many crocs become quite skillful at snapping up raindrops!

NILE CROCODILE *Crocodylus niloticus*

Joe McDonald, TOM STACK AND ASSOCIATES

Kerry T. Givens, TOM STACK AND ASSOCIATES

THORNY DEVIL *Molloch horridus*

LEGENDARY LIZARDS

This incredibly spiked and spiny Australian lizard was named after an ancient god of child sacrifice. The name is quite inappropriate though, because the *Molloch horridus* is only eight inches (20cm) long and eats only ants—1,500 per meal!

The thorny protuberances all over the lizard's body aren't there just for defense: They're arranged in such a way that dew or rain is gradually channelled down the valleys until it gets to the THORNY DEVIL's mouth. Nice feature for a desert dweller!

BY THE WAY . . .

Lizards have long tails—snakes, short ones!

D. Barker, TOM STACK AND ASSOCIATES

SALAMANDER *Eurycea bilineata*

HOW HOT IS HOT?

The word SALAMANDER is a general name for an entire group of creatures that includes newts and sirens (pages 35 and 45). These amphibians look like moist lizards with long tails but no scales or claws. Their legs are so short that their bellies drag on the ground. Salamanders can grow back almost any body part—arms, legs, tails, even eye retinas and severed optic nerves. Some people call them "spring lizards," because they are often seen around natural springs.

Even today some people believe that the bite of the bright-colored salamander is the "kiss of death"! Here's some news for you: Salamanders have quite small teeth and don't bite hard, don't sting and don't have fangs. But they do have a fiery liquid called salamindrin that comes out of the pores located behind their ears. It's not a good idea to get this burning, nasty stuff in your eyes or mouth or in a cut, but if you're smart enough not to stick a salamandered finger up your nose, no harm will come from picking up the lizard lookalike.

NEWTS TO YOU

The newt looks a lot like the salamander but its life is more complicated. Instead of having the usual amphibian two-stage life cycle, it has three stages!

As the newly hatched larva of the RED-SPOTTED NEWT grows, it soon transforms into a creature called an eft. The lizard-shaped eft leaves its watery home for a life on the land. Warning, warning! The eft's beautiful red skin—unusually rough and dry for an amphibian—is poisonous! Most animals are smart enough to steer clear of it. The eft's only real worry is skunks, which simply tear the eft apart and, skipping the poison skin, eat only the insides. Eventually, after several years, the eft's skin changes again to a smooth, slick, greenish brown, non-toxic covering. The tail grows broad and flat for swimming and the red-spotted newt returns to the larval pond of its youth to live out its remaining days!

BY THE WAY . . .

In Shakespeare's day the witches in *Macbeth* used "eye of newt" (the toxic skin secretions) to make their evil brew!

RED-SPOTTED NEWT *Notophthalmus viridescens*

David M. Dennis, TOM STACK AND ASSOCIATES

John Cancalosi, TOM STACK AND ASSOCIATES

CANE TOAD *Bufo marinus*

LOADS OF TOADS

It's a really big deal for any country to lose one of its principal crops, and that's exactly what was happening to the sugar crop in Australia in 1935. The hungry cane beetle was eating every bit of sugarcane it could get, so the growers brought in 100 CANE TOADS from Hawaii, in hopes that they would live up to their reputation and eat the cane beetles before any more damage was done. No such luck! The eight-inch (20.3cm) toads ignored the beetles and concentrated on snakes and frogs. Now the toads are everywhere, busily laying 54,000 eggs at a time. If anything or anyone tries to eat them, they promptly secrete a poison potent enough to kill a dog in 15 minutes. Now there's a real mess—as often happens when people try to fool with Mother Nature, the problem is compounded!

DID YOU KNOW . . .

Most toads secrete a milky toxin from a gland behind their eyes. If any creatures take a bite of them, they have to spit out the burning mouthful!

SURPRISINGLY ENOUGH . . .

Toads eat their own shed skin for the valuable nutrients contained in it!

CAN YOU IMAGINE . . .

When confronted by a hungry snake, clever toads gulp air into their stomach and intestines, blowing themselves up too big to be swallowed!

Chip Isenhart, TOM STACK AND ASSOCIATES

BY THE WAY . . .

Of the mother toad's thousands of eggs, only 10 may make it to adulthood!

Matt Bradley, TOM STACK AND ASSOCIATES

LOGGERHEAD *Caretta caretta*

IT'S THE OCEAN LIFE FOR ME

The big sea turtles spend most of their lives in the ocean, where their heavy, 300- to 1,500-pound (136–681kg) shapes become amazingly graceful supported by the water. Some of the turtles are called LOGGERHEADS. They nest on beaches around the world. In the United States from April to August, the nomads come close to the shore on both coasts to feed around the reefs and rocks guarding the nesting beaches. Swimming mostly with their front flippers, the turtles can home in on the short section of any nesting beach that they prefer.

The female doesn't have to rush, since she has the ability to lay her eggs up to six years after fertilization! But once she is ready to do it, she waits until dark to start the slow trek onto the sand, lugging her huge body 300 feet (92m) up the beach past the high-tide line.

If you should ever be lucky enough to see this event, don't even think of petting the large lady. For one thing, you'd probably scare her back into the water and no eggs would be laid (worse for her). Or (worse for you) she'd live up to her name in Sri Lanka—"Dog Turtle"—and bite your finger off!

Once she's made it to the nesting site, she's got to finish her task and get back in the water before dawn when birds, dogs and beachcombers will come along and find the secret nest. Thirty minutes are spent shovelling out a six-inch (15cm) deep hole as big as her body. Then the hind flippers dig down eight more inches (20cm) to form the egg pit. Legend says that she'll be "crying," because of her offsprings' risky future. In reality, the thick fluid oozing from her eyes keeps them clean and rids her kidneys of excess salt. The eggs themselves fall down into the prepared hole. They're tough, not brittle like hens eggs, but rubbery and flexible. Thirty more minutes to lay the 120 eggs and the concealment begins. She has to fill the egg-pit and then the body hole with sand. Finally, she must disturb and scatter the surrounding sand in every direction, to hide any traces.

BY THE WAY . . .

When the baby turtles hatch 8–10 weeks later, they make a midnight dash for their home in the ocean. The males will most likely *never* set foot on land again!

At last the mother turtle returns to the sea. She will probably come back on land again three to ten times this breeding season and lay up to 800 eggs. Then, exhausted from the effort, she'll take several years off.

Joe/Carol McDonald, TOM STACK AND ASSOCIATES

COPPERHEAD *Agkistrodon contortrix*

THE ART OF BEING INVISIBLE

Many snakes, especially the "ambush" vipers, rely on the camouflage-coloration of their skin to avoid being seen. There's no way, for instance, to spot a COPPERHEAD lying motionless in a pile of autumn leaves!

The snake's outer skin is made of **keratin**, a substance like fingernails, which has thickened and formed scales. Unlike our skin, the snake's doesn't grow along with its body, so the snake has to change its skin—sometimes four times a year—to keep up with its own growth. The process, called **molting**, actually starts days before the main event takes place. The copperhead's body starts to look dull and lifeless and its eyes get cloudy. It becomes irritable and loses its appetite. Finally, the big day arrives! The copperhead rubs its mouth on a rough surface until the skin comes loose. Slowly, like turning a sock inside out, it wriggles out of its skin. The new skin is much brighter and, of course, looser—to accommodate future new growth. What's left behind is a complete piece of inside-out old skin, right down to and including the eye coverings!

DID YOU KNOW . . .

Molting can take minutes, a half hour, or even days!

AMAZING AS IT SOUNDS . . .

A completely severed snake head can still bite a half hour later!

David M. Dennis, TOM STACK AND ASSOCIATES

GILA MONSTER *Heloderma suspectum*

POISONOUS PETS

Only two out of more than 3,000 lizards are poisonous! The GILA MONSTER, living in the arid regions of Mexico and the southwestern United States, is one of them. Now, why would anyone want a poisonous lizard for a pet, especially considering some of the awful stories that have been told about it. For example:

- The gila monster is a cross between a lizard and a crocodile. (It's not.)
- It's poisonous because it can't get rid of body waste. (No, it's poisonous, all right, but this is the wrong reason.)
- It has really bad breath, for the same reason. (Still wrong!)
- It leaps on its victim, spits venom from its poisonous tongue and is quite impossible to kill! (All untrue.)

Sound like good enough reasons *not* to keep a gila monster around the house? Nevertheless, by 1952 so many gila monsters had been sold as pets that they were close to extinction and placed on the endangered list!

Kevin Schafer/Martha Hill, TOM STACK AND ASSOCIATES

GREEN TREE PYTHON *Chondropython viridus*

TAKING MATTERS INTO HER OWN COILS

By basking in the sun or sheltering in the shade, most reptiles are able to achieve a body temperature of as much as 30°F warmer—or cooler—than the surrounding air. The GREEN TREE PYTHON is one of an amazing group of snakes (including the Indian and Blood pythons) that are able to produce heat on their own! This very special trait is used for only one purpose: to care for the creature's eggs. This ability allows the python to live in a cooler climate than some other egg-laying snakes.

After she lays her eggs, the female python wraps her coils around the **clutch** and stays put for months, instead of slithering off like most snakes do. By intense shivering, she is able to raise her body temperature up to 13°F (7°C)—high enough to keep the eggs at the heat they need to develop. Unfortunately, their mother will lose half her body weight from the effort, and it will take her three to five years to recover enough to try it again.

BY THE WAY . . .

Once the eggs hatch, it's business as usual and the hatchlings are on their own!

GOING HOME

By some miracle of nature, GREEN SEA TURTLES, which feed off the eastern coast of South America, navigate across the Atlantic Ocean to Ascension Island, three-quarters of the way and 1400 miles towards Africa, for nesting! How do they do it? Scientists believe that they may have several means of finding their way: Along the coast they simply follow the shoreline. In the open ocean they may use the sun as a compass, or possibly, landmarks on the ocean floor. Magnetically sensitive particles in their brains could be responding to the earth's magnetic field. Or, is it possible they are "smelling" the ocean currents and the odor of far-off lands?

Joe McDonald, TOM STACK AND ASSOCIATES

GREEN SEA TURTLE *Chelonia mydas*

INCREDIBLE, BUT . . .

It will be 40 years before the newly hatched green turtles return to the nesting beaches!

Dave B. Fleetham, TOM STACK AND ASSOCIATES

Celestial navigation is not likely, because turtle eyesight is adapted for underwater vision and they are quite nearsighted out of water. You can see that if turtles are indeed "sniffing" their way home, ocean **pollution** could be disastrous for this already endangered species!

FROGS AND TOADS

Frogs are kind of cute, but nobody seems very fond of the warty TOAD. You know the difference, don't you? Frogs have smooth, moist skin, long, specialized legs for leaping and toe pads for climbing. Toads, on the other hand, seem to have drier, bumpy skin; they're more short-legged and heavy-set, with a prominent, rounded poison-producing gland located below the ears.

There are about 3,800 species of hoppers and they live everywhere except for the polar regions, Greenland and some oceanic islands. The GOLDEN TOAD is found only in the Monteverde Cloud Forest in Costa Rica, where it is never seen except for the few days each year that it comes out to find a mate. Its last appearance was in 1987—no one's seen it since! Where is it hiding? Is it extinct? This is another of nature's mysteries.

Rod Planck, TOM STACK AND ASSOCIATES

AMERICAN TOAD *Bufo americanus*

John Cancalosi, TOM STACK AND ASSOCIATES

GOLDEN TOAD *Bufo periglenes*

THE UGLIEST SIREN YOU EVER SAW

The sirens of Greek mythology were beautiful, sweet-singing water nymphs. These SIRENS, on the other hand, look like eels with stubby front legs. They don't say much—just croak a bit—and, like "Peter Pan," they never grow up, staying for all their lives in the infantile larval form. These eternally juvenile amphibians live in the southeastern United States in shallow rivers and ditches, eating worms, snails and algae.

AMAZINGLY . . .

Not only do sirens have both feathery gills on the outside of their body and lungs on the inside, but they can also breathe through their skin!

Sirens are always coated with a slippery, slimy soap-like mucus that makes them almost impossible to hold on to. If the rains don't come and the old watering hole dries up, sirens survive by digging down a foot (.3m) or so in the mud and going to sleep for a couple of months. Their mucus coating turns into a hard covering that protects them by completely sealing in their remaining body moisture!

David M. Dennis, TOM STACK AND ASSOCIATES

DWARF SIREN *Pseudobrachus striatus*

FASTER THAN A SPEEDING BULLET

To a bug a "safe" distance away, the CHAMELEON looks harmless enough. In fact, the potential snack probably doesn't even *see* the camouflaged chameleon until the lizard's tongue shoots out of its mouth faster than your eye can follow. How does it do that? The tongue is hollow, like a straw. It bunches up in the chameleon's mouth the way an accordion closes, and it fires with the speed of a bullet—in only 1/100th of a second! The tongue is actually longer than the lizard! At the end of it is a sticky bulb of glue-like stuff that is capable of holding on to a meal of insects and sometimes a small animal.

Like the anole, this master of disguise can blend in perfectly with its surroundings, even becoming blotched with color to merge into the background. Specialized cells called "chromatophores" make it possible. Now where did that bug go?

WOULD YOU BELIEVE . . .

Chameleon eyes are set on the tip of cone-like turrets that swivel around independent of each other. That allows the chameleon to look in two directions at once!

JACKSON'S CHAMELEON *Chameleo jacksoni*

Chip/Jill Isenhart, TOM STACK AND ASSOCIATES

John Cancalosi; TOM STACK AND ASSOCIATES

TEXAS HORNED TOAD *Phrynosoma cornutum*

A THORN IN THE THROAT

Even snakes don't try to eat the TEXAS HORNED TOAD. It's really a lizard that lives in North and Central America from southern Canada to Panama. It's so spiked and spiny that if its spines were to get stuck in the snake's throat, it would be "curtains" for the snake! The toad's favorite food is ants; it loves them and eats them whenever it can. Then spiky runs back to its underground home. Any animal catching it out in the open is in for a big surprise. The startled horned toad has a scare tactic of its own! It puffs right up, restricting the blood flow out of its head, raising the pressure and bursting the delicate capillaries in its eyes. Out squirts the blood! Look out! Its aim is right on target up to seven feet (2.1m)!

AS A MATTER OF FACT . . .

Horned toads love barren desert habitats; some can withstand temperatures up to 116°F (47°C)!

BY THE WAY . . .

Not only do lizards have an upper eyelid—but most come with a lower one, too! It's transparent to keep out burrs, thorns and dust.

John Cancalosi, TOM STACK AND ASSOCIATES

GREY-BANDED KING SNAKE *Lampropeltis mexicana*

WHO'S KING OF THE HILL?

There are lots of poisonous snakes out there—rattlesnakes, coral snakes, mambas, taipans, water moccasins—but none of them are "top-dog." Why? Because the KING SNAKE is. It may seem harmless to us, but it eats poisonous snakes by the bushel!

SURPRISINGLY . . .

Snakes don't have to open their mouths to flick their tongues. They have a notch in the upper lip to put it through!

You see, it's immune to their venom. King snakes are constrictors; that means they disable their intended dinner by suffocating it—even other snakes.

The constrictor does not kill by crushing. Instead, every time the victim breathes out, the snake tightens its coils, preventing the ribs from expanding again. Pretty soon there's no room in the victim's chest for air. Goodbye, prey!

DID YOU KNOW . . .

Female snakes are almost always larger than males!

CAN YOU IMAGINE . . .

Some snakes have 400 vertebrae—humans only have 33!

Occasionally, nature will pull a fast one and a very unusual animal will be born, as in the case of the two-headed snake. It was doing just fine until the day when Head #1 decided that Head #2 would make an easy snack and tried to swallow it. Observers rescued Head #2 only to have it later take revenge on Head #1, with fatal results for both heads and the shared body!

RATSNAKE *Elaphe obsoleta*

Robert C. Simpson, TOM STACK AND ASSOCIATES

Joe McDonald, TOM STACK AND ASSOCIATES

EASTERN DIAMONDBACK RATTLESNAKE *Crotalus adamanteus*

ARMED AND DANGEROUS

Copperheads, water moccasins and rattlers are all venomous snakes. Their poison-delivery teeth are so long that they have to fold back into a sheath of skin in the mouth to keep from sticking *themselves!* A snake's fangs are so important to its survival that it always has a spare growing alongside the old tooth.

RATTLESNAKES are known for their habit of

INTERESTINGLY . . .

One group of rattlers that live on an island in the Gulf of California with no population of large animals have lost their rattles!

shaking the rattles on their tails. This defensive maneuver keeps the snake from getting stepped on and accidentally injured by a large animal—a cow, for instance. The rattles are made of keratin, a substance similar to human fingernails. Each one of the loosely interlocked shells was once a scale that has enlarged and thickened. Every time the snake sheds its skin (molts), a scale is retained and a new rattle is formed. The rattles hit against each other, making the characteristic buzzing sound. Depending on the size of the snake, the rattling can be heard from three to 160 yards (.9–49m) away!

LEGEND HAS IT . . .

Rattlers coil clockwise in the Northern Hemisphere and counterclockwise in the Southern!

By the way, don't bother to try to guess how old a snake is from the number of rattles. Some snakes shed as many as four times a year. Besides, rattles wear out and break off all the time. Usually, a wild snake has no more than 14, though, in its own best interests, eight is perhaps the ideal number for maximum sound and effect.

Brian Parker, TOM STACK AND ASSOCIATES

SURPRISINGLY . . .

Rattlesnakes don't always rattle before striking, but when they're annoyed they may rattle for hours!

David M. Dennis, TOM STACK AND ASSOCIATES

EGG-EATING SNAKE *Dasypeltis scabra*

ONE WAY TO EAT AN EGG

Unlike lizards, snakes can't tear their food into bite-sized pieces to eat it. Their only choice is to swallow it whole and they do, amazing human observers with the enormous size of some of their dinners. The African EGG-EATING SNAKE is able to swallow a smooth bird's egg twice as large as itself! Even though we think of eggs as delicate and brittle, their oval shape makes them surprisingly resistant to damage and crushing. The snake's feat is like bobbing for apples without using your hands, but in a way the egg-eating snake has an even bigger problem—it has almost no teeth! So, how does it grab hold of the slippery egg? In place of teeth are thick folds of muscular gum tissue. The folds act like suction cups pulling the egg steadily into the snake's mouth. Now, how to get *inside* the egg! As the egg starts down the snake's throat, sharp projections that stick out of the snake's backbone pierce the shell and the liquid inside flows down into the snake's belly. The remaining, but useless, shell is neatly compressed and regurgitated all in one piece!

WHO'S GOT A HOLE IN THE HEAD?

A GECKO, that's who! One African species has such thin skin and straight ear openings that you can see light coming right through from the other side of its head! From the smallest one-inch (2.54cm) long to the largest 14-inch (35.5cm), geckos can cling to almost any surface. No, they don't have suction-cup feet! But they do have fine ridges and tiny bristles that cover their soles. These bristles fill every nook and cranny of the surface that the gecko is climbing on and hold it in place. To let go, the gecko curls its toes and releases the tension that is keeping it attached. This is a very practical asset when chasing a buggy dinner up the wall!

Brian Parker, TOM STACK AND ASSOCIATES

MADAGASCAR DAY GECKO *Phelsuma dubia*

David M. Dennis, TOM STACK AND ASSOCIATES

MADAGASCAR LEAF GECKO *Uroplatus fimbriatus*

STRANGELY ENOUGH . . .

Geckos twitch their tails just like cats before lunging at prey!

BELIEVE IT OR NOT . . .

The Tokay Gecko (*Gecko gecko*) named itself by the sound it makes: "Gecko, gecko!"

Cristopher Crowley, TOM STACK AND ASSOCIATES

MARINE IGUANA *Amblyrhynchus cristatus*

WATER DRAGON

The volcanic Galapagos Islands, west of South America in the Pacific Ocean, straddle the Equator. It's blisteringly hot on the land and bracingly cold in the water, brought up from the Antarctic by the Humboldt Current. Here lives the only lizard completely adapted to life in the sea. The MARINE IGUANA isn't really that good a swimmer, but it is a fabulous diver! It uses its flattened tail to submerge down to 45 feet (13.7m) when it goes after the short reddish limestone-rich algae that it eats.

Each Galapagos island has its own type of marine iguana, isolated by water from the others. There are eight kinds in all, easily recognized by their different colors. The differences have evolved because, even though these iguanas are at home in the water, they will not swim the distance to the other islands! Scientists think the lizards must have floated to the isolated islands on driftwood "boats." When they didn't find normal lizard food (insects and such) on the geologically "new" volcanic islands, they took to the water in search of something to eat!

STRANGELY ENOUGH . . .

When the marine iguana's eggs hatch, there are equal numbers of males and females, but by adulthood there are far more females. Scientists guess it's because the males dive deeper than the females—right down to where the sharks cruise!

These lizards aren't lonely: The friendly, fun-loving sea lions are the iguanas' constant companions. Talk about two different personalities! The sea lion loves to annoy the lizard. The seal's idea of a good time is to poke and prod a sunning iguana until it tries to escape by running for the water. And that's exactly what the sea lion wants! It follows the lizard into the ocean, pulling on its tail and playing "cat and mouse" with it. Don't worry! The dragon is never hurt—only its dignity is wounded!

THE LIZARD IS A LADY

Reptiles, like all animals, have many different ways of protecting themselves. Some, like the chameleon, use color as camouflage, automatically blending in with their surroundings. Some, like the Dart Poison Frog, use their bright colors as a warning, signalling danger to their enemies. Others, like the Komodo Dragon or the rattlesnake, use their size or poison to stand their ground, prepared to fight.

One little Australian lizard that lives in the tropic woodlands has a different defense tactic. Along its neck lie deep folds of extra skin, supported by thin bony ribs. When facing trouble, the FRILLED LIZARD throws its head back, opens it mouth and blasts the huge—almost as large as its whole body—neck ruff open. This surprise display has the same effect as a lady popping open her parasol in the face of an pesky suitor. The result? Stunned shock—giving the lady (or the lizard) time to make a hasty retreat!

BESIDES THAT . . .

Frilled lizards also use their ruffs to bluff their opponents into thinking that they're bigger than they really are!

FRILLED LIZARD *Clamydosaurus kingii*

John Cancalosi, TOM STACK AND ASSOCIATES

John Cancalosi, TOM STACK AND ASSOCIATES

YELLOW ANACONDA *Eunectes notaeus*

SUPER SERPENT

This is it—the snake that nightmares are made of! The South American ANACONDA, a member of the boa family, is usually about 18 feet (5.2m) long, but once in a while a snake is found that is double that length!

ON THE OTHER HAND . . .

The Taruma Indians believe that the anaconda is a kind soul that turns itself into a beautiful ship with white sails every evening. And that they are descended from it!

An average-size anaconda can kill and eat a full-sized caiman (a South American crocodilian). How can it do that! It's simple for this super serpent. It hunts in two ways. Hanging out around the edge of the sluggish, swampy water it prefers, occasionally dangling from a tree, the snake waits patiently until a rodent, bird, deer, or whatever comes along for a drink. Then ZAP! It grabs the unlucky prey in its mouth and drags it to the bottom of the pond to drown it.

If that doesn't work, anacondas go out looking for food. Whatever it catches gets wrapped in its coils and squeezed until it can't breathe anymore. Then comes the interesting part. Like all snakes, the anaconda swallows its meal whole! Yes, even a deer! By unhinging its jaw, it can open its mouth wide enough for really huge prey to fit in headfirst—even if the victim is larger around than the snake's body *and* even if it's still alive and kicking! Wow, that's an almost unbelievable picture! And the snake handles it all with ease! Not only is its brain encased in bone to protect it, but there's also a valve on the breathing tube that allows it to go right on breathing, despite the large object squeezing down its throat!

A caiman will take a week or more to digest, and a meal that large can last the snake up to a year, if nothing else happens along. Naturally, there are plenty of horror stories about humans disappearing—victims of the "wowlah" (one of the anaconda's local names). Well, there's only been one *documented* case of a human being taken. The proof consisted of strangulation marks on the body, and the snake had not made any attempt to swallow the person. But that doesn't take into account all the *unexplained* mysterious disappearances in anaconda country!

THE FROG THAT PREDICTS THE WEATHER

Spadefoot toads are nicknamed RAIN FROGS even though they don't live anywhere near water. Some even live in desert sand dunes. So how did they get their name? They came to be known as rain frogs because people thought they could actually predict rain! Before a shower hundreds of toads would start calling, burping out their weather forecast, "Rain-today, rain-today." Some African farmers believe rain frogs don't just forecast, but actually *control* the weather. A dry season means especially good care for the hoppers!

DID YOU KNOW . . .

Spadefoot toads get their name from the spade-like shape of their back feet. What do you think they're used for? Right—shovelling sand!

SPADEFOOT TOAD *Scaphiopus couchi*

David M. Dennis, TOM STACK AND ASSOCIATES

Glossary

aborigine. A member of the original race that lived in a region such as an Aborigine of Australia.

algae. Any of a large group of plants that contain chlorophyll but are not divided into roots, stems and leaves.

autotomy. The breaking off of a damaged or trapped body part: the tail of a lizard, claw of a crab.

behavioral temperature control. Influencing internal body temperature by specific actions.

bromeliad. A plant of the pineapple family.

carnivorous. Flesh-eating.

celestial navigation. Navigation by the apparent position of heavenly bodies.

clutch. A group of eggs incubated at the same time.

dewlap. Hanging fold of skin under the neck of some animals.

echolocation. The sonar-like system used by dolphins, bats and other animals to detect objects around them through high-pitched sounds that are reflected and returned to the sensory organ of the sender.

epiphytical. Non-parasitic plant that grows above the ground or another plant or structure, obtaining nutrients from the air, rain and dust.

fossil. A trace or print of the remains of a plant or animal of a past age, preserved in earth or rock.

Galapagos. A group of islands west of South America in the Pacific Ocean, straddling the equator.

hibernate. To spend the winter in a dormant condition.

hormone. Any internally secreted compound formed in the endocrine glands that affects specifically receptive organs.

Ice Age. The Pleistocene epoch (two million to 10,000 years ago), when sheet ice moved across the northern hemisphere.

invertebrates. Animals without backbones.

keratin. A tough, insoluble protein that is the main constituent of hair, nails, horns, and hoofs.

larvae. The young of an animal that undergoes metamorphosis.

lichen. An organism composed of both algae and fungus cells that are

Jeff Foott, TOM STACK AND ASSOCIATES

POLAR BEAR
Ursus maritimus

usually dependent on each other for survival. Resembling a moss, lichen has no leaves, stems or roots.

lobe. A rounded part of an ear. The projection at the end of an elephant's trunk.

mammoth. A very large, hairy, extinct elephant with tusks that curved upwards.

marsupial. A mammal that gives birth to tiny, poorly developed young, which it carries in a pouch on the mother's stomach (kangaroo, opossum, and so on).

metabolism. The process by which a living being uses food to obtain energy, build tissue and dispose of waste.

metamorphosis. A profound change in form from one stage to the next in the life history of an organism.

molting. Casting or shedding the feathers, skin or the like in the process of renewal or growth.

monotreme. An egg-laying mammal of the order Monotremata, now restricted to New Guinea and Australia—olatypus and spiny anteater (echidna).

mucus. A sticky, slippery substance. In humans, it is usually produced by membranes in the nose and throat.

pit viper. Any of various vipers that have a heat-sensitive pit above each nostril.

placental. A mammal that retains the fertilized egg in its body until an advanced state of development is reached.

pollution. The introduction of harmful substances into the environment.

predator. An animal that lives mostly by killing and eating other animals.

prehensile. Able to grasp things, the way a monkey's tail can; adapted for seizing, grasping or taking hold of.

radar. A radio device for detecting the position of things in the distance and the direction of moving objects.

Seychelles. A group of islands and inlets located in the Indian Ocean about 900 miles (1,450km) off the coast of Africa.

sonar. A method for detecting and locating things underwater by echolocation.

tadpoles. Larvae of frogs and toads.

TSD (temperature-dependent sex determination). Offspring's sex determined by outside temperature rather than other factors.

vertebrates. Animals with backbones.

D. Barker, TOM STACK AND ASSOCIATES

BUSH VIPER *Atheris squamigera*